THIS IS
CHRISTIANITY

THIS IS
CHRISTIANITY

Maxie Dunnam

ABINGDON PRESS
Nashville

THIS IS CHRISTIANITY

Copyright © 1994 by Abingdon Press

This is Christianity: Leader's Guide,
Prepared by John Schroeder
Copyright © 1994 by Abingdon Press

This book is printed on recycled, acid-free paper.

Library of Congress Cataloging-in-Publication Data

Dunnam, Maxie D.
   This is Christianity / Maxie Dunnam.
     p.   cm.
   Includes bibliographical references.
   ISBN 0-687-08410-5 (pbk : alk. paper)
   1. Theology, Doctrinal—Popular works. 2. Christian life.
I. Title.
BT77.D76   1994
230—dc20   94-12639
                                                  CIP

Scripture quotations, unless otherwise indicated, are from the New Revised Standard Version Bible, copyright © 1989, by the Division of Christian Education of the National Council of the Churches of Christ in the United States of America.

Scripture quotations noted JB are from *The Jerusalem Bible,* copyright © 1966 by Darton, Longman & Todd, Ltd. and Doubleday & Company, Inc. Used by permission of the publishers.

Scripture quotations noted JBP are from *The New Testament in Modern English,* by J. B. Phillips. Copyright © 1972 by Macmillan Publishing Co., Inc.

Scripture quotations noted KJV are from the King James Version of the Bible.

Scripture quotations noted NEB are from *The New English Bible.* © The Delegates of the Oxford University Press and the Syndics of the Cambridge University Press 1961, 1970. Reprinted by permission.

Scripture quotations noted NIV are taken from the *Holy Bible: New International Version.* Copyright © 1973, 1978, 1984 by the International Bible Society. Used by permission of Zondervan Bible Publishers.

Scripture quotations noted NKJV are from the The New King James Version. Copyright © 1979, 1980, 1982, Thomas Nelson, Inc., Publishers.

Scripture quotations noted RSV are from the Revised Standard Version of the Bible, copyright 1946, 1952, 1971 by the Division of Christian Education of the National Council of Churches of Christ in the USA. Used by permission.

Some Scripture quotations are the author's own paraphrase.

97 98 99 00 01 02 03 04 — 10 9 8 7 6 5 4

MANUFACTURED IN THE UNITED STATES OF AMERICA

To
Kimberly Lynn
Kerry Leigh
Gerald Kevin

*   *   *

once and always my children—now my friends.

*   *   *

And to
John David Reisman
Jason Lee Peeples

*   *   *

Children by marriage—also my friends.

ACKNOWLEDGMENTS

This book is not my own doing. My daughter, the Reverend Kimberly Reisman, played a major role in research, outline, and content. She shared with me in listening groups as we heard questions from people at all stages of Christian growth and concern.

Dr. Craig Gallaway has been my consulting theologian. He has "forced" clear thinking, and saved me from too many inconsistencies and sloppily expressed ideas.

The following played special roles in conversation groups, reading and responding as the material was developed: Andy and Lilli Ann Hirsh, Skip and Stacey Burzumato, Melissa Neyland, Rich Cook, Kirk Bailey, Don Bourland, and Phil Connolly.

The entire staff of Christ United Methodist Church in Memphis, Tennessee, played a significant role in the preparation of this manuscript. Much of this material was presented to them in its initial stages for their reflection and feedback. Their response helped shape the present content.

I'm grateful to all of these, and to Mary K. Marino, my Administrative Assistant/Secretary for more than ten years, for again going above and beyond the call of duty in word processing and manuscript preparation.

CONTENTS

INTRODUCTION

As I was wrestling with the idea of writing this book, I had an appointment with a young Jewish man who wanted to talk with me about the Christian faith. In a series of conferences with him, I discovered that he was not interested in theological discussions and debates, not interested in complicated theology or theology-become-philosophy. Rather, he wanted a kind of ABC's of the Christian faith, the foundational beliefs, the basic content of the Christian faith, expressed as simply as possible. I did with him what I have done with countless other folks. I did not pursue an explanation of complex theological propositions; rather, I explored relationships and their meaning for our lives.

All religion is an effort to understand and to give expression to our relationships with God. No matter how we talk about it, that is our struggle. As human beings, we are incurably religious, and we want to understand more fully the deep and mysterious relationship between God and the world, between God and us human beings.

So I accepted the challenge to write a Christian primer. Let the reader be clear that this book is a primer. I see my audience in three groups. The first group includes persons who are not a part of the Church, who may not even be interested in the Church in any kind of institutional way, but who want to explore the basic teachings of the Christian faith. The second group includes persons who are interested in the Church but have not yet embraced the faith of the Church. They find meaning in some relationship with the Church, however tentative that relationship may be; but they are now only at the doorway of the Church, looking in. Then there is the third group: persons who are in the Church, participating in the life of a congregation, although they may have little knowledge of the basic content of the faith. Surveys have revealed that many people active in the Church—Sunday school teachers, leaders of the institutional life of the congregation, including long-time members of the Church—are many times confused and uncertain about the basic doctrines of the Christian faith. They have become so involved in the life of the Church, so much a part of it, that they are hesitant to express their lack of knowledge, their limitation in understanding and/or communicating the elementary truths of the faith.

This book is not an effort to convince the reader of the validity of the Christian faith. It is a witness, a commentary on basic Christianity, an effort to answer persons who are asking elementary questions about the Christian faith.

Religious educator and editor Martin Marty suggests that the task of the Church has to do with both "coring and caring." The coring function of the Church is to provide clarity about the fundamentals of the faith, the ABC's of Christian doctrine. That necessitates a decision about what is the core of the Christian faith. It is my conviction, and thus the perspective of this book, that the core has been established in the classic creeds of the Church. A creed is the way the Church has chosen to talk about the faith.

Early in its life, when the Church was beset by pressures within and without to set forth its identity, there emerged a rule of faith, a simple statement of the fundamentals for persons making a first profession of faith, and for the general purpose of distinguishing between the basic Christian vision and its distortions. This became known as the Apostles' Creed:

I believe in God the Father Almighty,
    maker of heaven and earth;

And in Jesus Christ his only Son our Lord:
    who was conceived by the Holy Spirit,
        born of the Virgin Mary,
        suffered under Pontius Pilate,
        was crucified, dead, and buried;
        he descended into hell,
    the third day he rose from the dead;
    he ascended into heaven,
        and sitteth at the right hand of God the Father Almighty;
    from thence he shall come to judge the quick and the dead.

I believe in the Holy Spirit,
    the holy catholic church,
    the communion of saints,
    the forgiveness of sins,
    the resurrection of the body,
    and the life everlasting. Amen.

Later, this time in the midst of debate about the uniqueness of Christ, the Council of Nicaea drew up some definite articles of belief, which became the second great ecumenical foundation of belief called the Nicene Creed.

As theology educator and author Gabriel Fackre reminds us:

Subsequent eras produce their own statements of the story. All bear the marks of the time in which they were formed, from the substance philosophy that influences ancient confessions to the masculine language that dates many modern credos. But the translation and accommodation circle around and return to a core conviction. It is made up of refrains that run through the charter of the Christian religion, the Bible, and recur in the classic and contemporary formulations of the faith. They represent the abiding skeletal framework for the flesh and blood of any statement of faith. (Fackre, p. 15)

So it is that with which we will be dealing in this book—the core of the Christian faith, the skeletal framework of the dynamic that has kept the faith alive, kept it defined, and has claimed the commitment and allegiance of millions of people. Though I will elaborate on some of the expressions of the Apostles' Creed, this is not a commentary on the creed. It is a statement, in order and style, that I pray will be a helpful presentation of basic Christian beliefs and practical ways these beliefs express themselves in Christian living.

CHAPTER ONE

GOD THE FATHER ALMIGHTY

Who is God?

John was in his mid-twenties. He had fought addiction to alcohol and other drugs since his early teens. John's addiction had brought great frustration, struggle, and pain to his family, especially his mother and father. He was recovering and had had eighteen months of sobriety and freedom from drugs when he relapsed. John's shame and guilt were devastating. He entered a long period of deep, morbid depression. His primary concern was the love of his mother and father. Their word to him, repeated over and over again and acted out in every possible way, was, "We love you no matter what. You are our son. We love you whether you are sober or drunk, whether you are good or bad, whether you are a success or a failure. No matter what happens to you we are your parents, and we will never cease loving you."

This is the core of the Christian story. The biblical witness is to God's constant and faithful love of those who believe in God, despite their sin, failure, and inconstancy. The Apostles' Creed (printed on page 13) is accepted by all of Christendom as a foundation creed for the Christian faith. It begins, "I believe in God the Father Almighty, maker of heaven and earth." When we say, "I believe in God the Father Almighty," we are proclaiming our faith in just this kind of God.

God as Father

We begin our exploration of the Christian faith by reflecting on the image of God as Father. Like all images, metaphors, and names for God, father can be misinterpreted and even abused. We should not infer from this image, for example, that God has gender, or that every action of every earthly father is an adequate or accurate reflection of our heavenly Father. Nor should we infer that the actions of earthly mothers give us no insight into who God is. Indeed, in our opening story, the love of both the mother and the father gave us insight into who God is. Nevertheless, images are very important in communicating and understanding the Christian story. Images and the stories of which they are a part convey much more fully and truly than abstract concepts the reality of our relationship to God, which is the essence of our faith.

The primary reason we call God Father is that Jesus did so, and he taught us so to do. This is the controlling rule in our use of this image: We do not speak of God as Father, or seek to understand this image, apart from Jesus whom we speak of as "God the Son." Otherwise, we could miss the real point of Jesus' address, or we might see the designation Father as only a metaphor for Creator, when much more is imaged here. As Theodore W. Jennings, Jr., reminds us in his book *Loyalty to God*, the Christian cannot think about God as Father without connecting the image with the one who made it so powerfully real in the Christian story: Jesus of Nazareth.

With the coming of Christ, the meaning of God's fatherhood for the Christian faith has been established once and for all. Contemporary theologian James I. Packer expressed the significance of this in the following way:

What is a Christian? The question can be answered in many ways, but the richest answer I know is that a Christian is one who has God for his father. . . .

The revelation to the believer that God is his father is in a sense the climax of the Bible, just as it was a final step in the revelatory process which the Bible records. . . .

If you want to judge how well a person understands Christianity, find out how much he makes of the thought of being God's child, and having God as his father. If this is not the thought that prompts and controls his worship and prayers and his whole outlook on life, it means that he does not understand Christianity very well at all. For everything that Christ taught, everything that makes the New Testament new, . . . is summed up in the knowledge of the fatherhood of God. "Father" is the Christian name for God. (Friesen and Maxson, p. 251)

With the coming of Christ and the God that we see in Jesus, we find a reclaiming and a fulfillment of the Old Testament. Jesus chose the image of Father in particular to reclaim and fulfill the traditions.

Christians do well to remember that Jesus' scripture was the Old Testament. He did not claim to bring something totally new or different, but to fulfill. The Old Testament is full of gracious images of God. What was new with Jesus was his address to his Father. In the New Testament, Jesus describes God as Father at least 170 times, and Jesus never prays to God by any other title than Father.

Taking their cue from Jesus, the early Christians called God Father. This naming of God reflected their experience of God. In response to the disciples' request that he teach them to pray, Jesus said, "When you pray, say, 'Our Father . . . ' " (Matthew 6:9, paraphrase). He used the Aramaic word *Abba*, which is something like our term *Daddy*. In turn, the early Christians followed Jesus' example. The apostle Paul referred to God as Abba, and he translated that into the Greek term *Pater* for his Gentile converts. Since Paul's letters were among the earliest *written* documents, they provide evidence of how important the way of addressing God was to the first Christians.

In these letters of Paul, we encounter the decisive naming of God as Abba/Pater and the explanation of that name, which gives us the core expression of the Christian faith: "I believe in God the Father Almighty."

Here is perhaps the earliest written expression of it in the New Testament:

> But they remain under guardians and trustees until the date set by the father. So with us; while we were minors, we were enslaved to the elemental spirits of the world. But when the fullness of time had come, God sent his Son, born of a woman, born under the law, in order to redeem those who were under the law, so that we might receive adoption as children. And because you are children, God has sent the Spirit of his Son into our hearts, crying, "Abba! Father!" So you are no longer a slave but a child and if a child then also an heir, through God. (Galatians 4:2-7)

Our Adoption

The significance of addressing God as "Abba! Father!" is enhanced by looking closely at this passage where the term occurs. Paul says that "while we were minors, we were enslaved to the elemental spirits of the world." Most translations of Scripture have "while we were children." "Elemental spirits" is Paul's designation for a variety of religious rules or philosophical practices by which people attempted then—and attempt now—to deal with the struggles and uncertainties of life and destiny.

The point Paul is trying to make is that when we were not yet mature, when we had not yet come into the Christian faith, we were "enslaved to the elemental spirits of the world"—various ways of trying to ensure our survival. The Greek word Paul uses can have several meanings. One is captured in the translation "elemental spirits." Paul could have been referring to the elements of which the world is composed, particularly the stars. The ancient world was haunted by a belief in astrology as a way of controlling one's destiny. As with those who follow astrological charts today, people tried to predict their futures—their sufferings and their hopes—by mapping the stars. The Bible commentator William Barclay suggests that the Greek word Paul uses can mean "a line of things," such as a file of soldiers.

Later, the Greek word came to mean any elementary body of teaching or knowledge, such as the ABC's (Barclay, pp. 37-38). In this second sense, the word can mean any system or set of rules whereby one seeks to control the forces and opportunities that impinge on life. In this regard, it is noteworthy that Paul also describes immaturity as a way of life "under the law." To be under the law in this sense is to try to use God's law apart from faith to establish one's own righteousness and standing in the community—a practice that Paul himself had known very well in his former life as a Pharisee.

Whatever particular meaning we choose for the Greek word, the overall impact of Paul's message is clear. Before Christ came to reveal who God is, all people lived as helpless children under the tyranny of the elemental forces of the universe, using the stars or laws or other methods to try to control, protect, and ensure destiny:

> But when the fullness of time had come, God sent his Son . . . in order to redeem those who were under the law, so that we might receive adoption as children. And because you are children, God has sent the Spirit of his Son into our hearts, crying, "Abba! Father!" (Galatians 4:4-6)

Theodore W. Jennings, Jr., writes that

> this acclamation is one which proclaims God as Father in both Aramaic and Greek. That is, whether in the language of Judaism (Abba) or in the language of paganism (Pater-Father), both Jew and Gentile respond to the proclamation that God is Father. God

is not the Father of one people, but of both peoples. (Jennings, p. 30)

As Paul asserted, "In Christ Jesus you are all sons of God. . . . There is neither Jew nor Greek" (Galatians 3:26, 28 RSV).

For a long time I missed the power of this dual designation: "Abba! Father!" The meaning is not simply that Jesus addressed the one whom we call Father in a more intimate way as Abba; the meaning is that two distinct peoples, Jews and Gentiles, are joined in the acclamation of God as Father. God has liberated us, set us free from slavery, adopted us as his children, and rescued us from all bondage. Whether we have tried to control our lives through following religious law (Jew) or through divining the stars and the order of nature (Greek), the message of Paul (and Jesus) is the same: The Father loves us. We no longer need to struggle with life— trying to find a way to control our fear or ensure our survival. The Father loves us. He holds our lives even beyond death. We can trust him.

I remember an experience when the notion of adoption by God became powerfully real to me. My wife, Jerry, and I were flying to Japan from Korea. When we were boarding the plane in Seoul, there were three young American servicemen who had in their care six tiny babies. In conversation we learned that an adoption agency was giving these young men a free trip home and back so that they might deliver the babies to American families.

Jerry, who is forever a mother, decided those young men needed help. They did appear rather helpless! So she volunteered to take one of the babies onto the plane and care for it until we reached Tokyo.

As the plane was taking off, I looked down at the little baby in Jerry's arms and was overcome with sadness. I thought, *She will never know her birth parents, will never know her homeland, perhaps will never visit here again, and will be forever separated from her birth family.*

Then I happened to look at the baby's arm and saw a little bracelet on it. I lifted the baby's hand and read on the bracelet Mr. and Mrs. John Mabry, followed by an address in Pittsburgh, Pennsylvania. *They have to be the adoptive parents to whom the baby is being delivered,* I thought. My sadness was transformed into happiness, even joy. I knew that in Pittsburgh were a man and a woman who had such love that they were willing to take the child as their own. And I knew that, all things being equal, the child would have the love and security that a mother and a father want to provide their children. Although that child would someday know the story of being adopted, long before that story would be known she would have experienced the love and care of the two parents. She would know the deep meaning of having been deliberately chosen, deliberately loved.

Suddenly, the notion of adoption by God became powerfully real to me. Adoption has to do with being secure in a relationship that is *given* to us. God is our Father—our Father who has adopted us, just as Mr. and Mrs. Mabry became the father and the mother of that little baby. He chooses us and claims us as his children. To be sure, as already asserted, we must remember that the designation of God as Father has nothing to do with gender: God is not a sexual being. Rather, it describes a relationship of shared love and fellowship in which God pours out all his blessings on all his children. In the deepest and truest sense we do not have to worry about our destiny or our survival by trying to divine or manipulate the elements of the universe: We have a Father who loves us and has adopted us.

What is perhaps Jesus' best-known parable, the parable of the prodigal son, gives us a vivid picture of what it means to be children of God.

Then Jesus said, "There was a man who had two sons. The younger of them said to his father, 'Father, give me the share of the property that will belong to me.' So he divided his property between them. A few days later the younger son gathered all he had and traveled to a distant country, and there he squandered his property in dissolute living. When he had spent everything, a severe famine took place throughout that country, and he began to be in need. So he went and hired himself out to one of the citizens of that country, who sent him to his fields to feed the pigs. He would gladly have filled himself with the pods that the pigs were eating; and no one gave him anything. But when he came to himself he said, 'How many of my father's hired hands have bread enough and to spare, but here I am dying of hunger! I will get up and go to my father, and I will say to him, "Father, I have sinned against heaven and before you; I am no longer worthy to be called your son; treat me like one of your hired hands."' So he set off and went to his father. But while he was still far off, his father saw him and was filled with compassion; he ran and kissed him. Then the son said to him, 'Father, I have sinned against heaven and before you; I am no longer worthy to be called your son.' But the father said to his slaves, 'Quickly bring out a robe—the best one—and put it on him; put a ring on his finger and sandals on his feet. And get the fatted calf and kill it, and let us eat and celebrate; for this son of mine was dead and is alive again; he was lost and is found!' And they began to celebrate!" (Luke 15:11-24)

What is the primary lesson? If we boil it down, refine it to its most precious essence, the central truth of the parable is this: When the prodigal son returned home, his father received him as though he had never been away.

Though Jesus teaches us much in the parable, most of all he gives us a picture of God. There is no mistaking the point: God, our Father, restores us to relationship. He exercises his power as Father. It is the power of forgiveness, love, and acceptance.

What is my relationship to God?

Gary Larson is a cartoonist I don't always understand. His cartoons are titled "The Far Side," and sometimes they are so far on the far side that I miss what he is trying to say.

However, I did get one cartoon. Larson depicted an over-stuffed woman seated on an overstuffed couch, hair in curlers, a broom in her right hand, and a telephone receiver in the left. She was surrounded by three large fish bowls, each containing a number of swimming creatures. She tells her friend that she kissed a frog, it turned into a prince, they got married—and wham! She's stuck at home "with a bunch of polliwogs!"

Most of us can identify with that in one way or another. Life sometimes seems a mess. We feel no connection. Relationships may seem superficial and shallow. Our primary relationships are often strained. We feel that we are stuck with "a bunch of polliwogs." To experience the reality that God has adopted us as children makes all the difference in the world.

The Love of the Father in Creation

To understand our adoption fully, we need to see that it is not somehow an afterthought of God. The grace we experience as adopted children, a love not earned or deserved but freely given, is a clue to God's purpose and intention toward us and all creation.

Creation itself provides the first clue to how God relates to the world and what it means to us and our adoption. Grace, the dynamic, radical love of God, is demonstrated in creation; in fact, creation is grace. To be sure, a lot of debate swirls around the notion of creation. But whether we follow a particular scientifically oriented concept of creation or give a literal interpretation to the creation story in Genesis, there remains a creative moment that is integral to the relationship between God and the world. The traditional belief that God created everything from nothing is very helpful because it describes the relationship between God and creation as one of *sheer generosity.*

Creation, then, is a radically free and creative act of love, producing something separate and different from God. Through this act of an utterly free love, something new and completely other is created. But this is not the whole story. The centerpiece of the overflow of God's love in creation is *another personal creature,* a living being in God's own image.

When we read the two creation stories in the first and second chapters of Genesis, we recognize that the act of creating is an extension of who God is.

Over against the ancient Greek philosophical notion that God exists in a kind of splendid isolation, Christian theologians have always emphasized God's care for and involvement in creation. Karl Barth explained that God does not will to be God without creation. The ancient writer Dionysius the Areopagite proclaimed that God creates the goodness of the world because God's goodness "yearns" to share the good.

God creates in Genesis because generosity is of his very nature. After each act of creation in bringing the world into being, the Genesis writer says, "And God saw that it was good." When all was finished with the creation of Adam and Eve, the response is, "It was *very* good."

God, in utterly free love, creates the world; and the climax of creation is man and woman:

> So God created humankind in his image, in the image of God he created them, male and female he created them. (Genesis 1:27)

The Love of the Father in Redemption

Yet God's work is not just a moment of creation but an ongoing commitment to that creation. God created the otherness of creation not in order to step back and watch it as a disinterested observer, but to be bound to it in a relationship of love, drawing the creature into the divine life and entering into the life of creation. Thus, in creating some thing, God also creates *relationship.* Though this relationship of love between God and creature begins with nothing, it continues as a creative process. Grace as seen in creation, then, is the continuous relationship of radically free love between God and creature, God and creation.

In other words, the Father creates out of love, and he also redeems. To speak of redemption (deliverance from something harmful by payment of a price) is to speak of sin and what has traditionally been called the Fall of humankind. The love of God in creation has been interrupted by sin and evil. We experience sin and evil today in many forms: not only in the crimes and violence that attack our neighborhoods and cities, but also in the greed, fear, and pride that infect our own lives. All of us are prodigals for whom the Father waits with love and forgiveness.

Imagine what our acceptance of this relationship can do to our sense of self-worth. William Glasser, known as the father of reality therapy, said that there are two basic needs in life: the need to love and be loved and the need to feel worthwhile to oneself and others. How difficult it is for us to accept ourselves, to love and be loved, to feel worthwhile to ourselves and others. It is a moment of almost overwhelming grace when we accept the fact that God knows us thoroughly and loves us unreservedly. To know that we are loved and accepted by God frees us to love ourselves and others and to know that we are of infinite worth. In this way our redemption (God's deliverance of us through Jesus' death on the cross) is also a moment of liberation.

Alex Haley's book *Roots* is the story of Kunta Kinte—the great-great-great-great-great-grandfather of Alex Haley—who had been taken as a slave in Africa and brought to this country. In one memorable scene in the book, Kunta Kinte drove his master to a ball at a big plantation house. He heard the music coming from inside the house, music from the white folks' instruments and the white folks' dance. He drew up the buggy in front of the house and settled down to wait out the long night as his master entered into the music and revelry. After a while, as he sat there in the buggy, he heard other music. As he listened, he realized that it was coming from the slaves' quarters behind the big house.

He listened. The music was different. Without even making the decision to move, he felt his legs carrying him down the path toward those cabins. There he found an elderly man playing music, African music, *his* music, which he remembered hearing when he was a child. It was music he had almost forgotten. In conversation, Kunta Kinte discovered that the man playing the music was from his section of Africa, and they talked excitedly in their native language.

Late that night, after returning from the dance, Kunta Kinte went home a changed man. Though he went to bed on the dirt floor of his little cabin, he was different. He wept in sadness, aware of what he had almost forgotten. He wept in joy, aware that at last he had remembered. The degrading, terrifying experience of slavery had almost destroyed him, almost obliterated his memory of who he was. The music had helped him remember.

What we call the gospel of Christ is God's music for the whole world. The apostle Paul says that this is what God in Christ does for us: "God sent forth his Son . . . to redeem. . . . So through God you are no longer a slave but a son" (Galatians 4:4-7 RSV).

This is a dramatic image. Paul is saying that human beings were formerly owned and ruled by forces under whose power they had become utterly powerless. They had, in fact, become resigned to their own condition. But God has not left us in this state of slavery. Our relationship to God liberates us from our bondage, helps us remember who we are created to be. Just as God liberated the Jews out of Egyptian bondage, so also God rescues and redeems us from whatever bondage may enslave us.

Perhaps the most radical thing that Paul says in this passage from Galatians is that we are no longer slaves at all; we have become children and heirs of God. That means that our relationship to God is not only liberation; it is also dignification.

When Paul talks about God adopting us and making us sons, he is talking about the elevation to dignity that God provides—restoring what had become hidden to its true value and worth. Paul's reference is not meant to be limited to sons in the strict sense, even though the word rendered "children" in recent translations of the New Testament is literally "sons." Daughters are included. Both male and female are liberated and dignified.

Though there has been much debate and confusion over this issue of male and female and their place in relation to God and in the Christian community, there is a sense in which the transformation of the status of the female Christian in New Testament times was even more dramatic than the transformation of the male. In the Christian community, by the grace of God, she is the equal of a son rather than being relegated to the traditional place of the daughter in that ancient culture.

Sons and daughters are made to be heirs of God. We are all set free, liberated from bondage, and dignified by our relationship to God.

How can I believe in a good God in a bad world?

In the Christian tradition, there has been an ongoing debate about which is more characteristic of God: sovereignty or love. If we put the emphasis on sovereignty (supreme power, dominion), we may end up with a doctrine of predestination, which restricts God's love to the election of particular people. If love is the defining characteristic of God, human beings are free and can accept or resist God's grace.

That is, we are not robots who have no decision to make about our destiny and our relation to God; we are free. Our freedom does not limit God's sovereignty and power; it underscores them. God could have created us without freedom to choose. But in power, defined by love, God gives us free will.

I believe that in the revelation of God that we have in Jesus, this is where we must begin—with love. We Christians do not define or explain God's love in terms of God's sovereignty; we define and explain God's sovereignty in terms of God's love. As Dionysius argued in the fourth century, God created us because God "yearned" to love us.

The question is then asked, Is God all-powerful? The answer is yes. God is all-powerful, almighty; but God's power is always defined, perhaps even limited, by love—by the almighty power of love. Because God is love, God does nothing to deny his love. The question persists: How can God be both all-powerful and all-loving?

The Father Almighty and Human Suffering

Perhaps the greatest challenge to faith in God's fatherly love and power is the human experience of pain and suffering. The question is often asked, If God is good (like a loving father) and also powerful (almighty), then why do innocent people (and other creatures) suffer? As C. S. Lewis understood, this way of putting the question tends to obscure a truly Christian grasp of the problem. In *The Problem of Pain*, Lewis acknowledged that Christians may never be able to resolve the question, but they still know how to pray, to seek God's comfort and assurance, to resist and protest the forces of evil, and to give one another encouragement in times of trouble and pain. This is the Christian response to suffering because it has always been God's response to the suffering of his people.

We must distinguish the almighty love of the Father from several false notions that may creep in as counterfeits. First of all, we must distinguish this kind of power and love from the coercive, callous, uncaring, unreliable, volatile, and dangerous earthly fathers that some have known. God the Father Almighty is not an abuser! Some feminist thinkers in our time have claimed that violence and abuse are inherent in the image of Father Almighty. But our survey of Jesus' teaching, especially the story of the prodigal son, has led us in a very different direction. Here is a portrait not of an abusive earthly father but of one who—though himself misused and terribly treated—still takes his child into the care, warmth, and protection of the family. To be sure, the prodigal has suffered; but this father is not the cause of the suffering. He is its cure.

Second, we must also distinguish the meaning of "Father Almighty" from any notion of automatic or magical deliverance from all pain and suffering. To trust our lives into the hands of God the Father is not to say that we shall never suffer. Indeed, the picture that we get of God throughout the Bible—Old and New Testaments—is not that God keeps his people in a place of no suffering, but that *he goes through their suffering with them so that it becomes redemptive.* This is the picture that we have of God from the time of Abraham, who suffered the uprooting of his family in order to follow the promise of God's blessing, to the time of Moses, who comforted and exhorted the people of Israel in the wilderness by reminding them that the God of Abraham, Isaac, and Jacob traveled with them. This is the God of Isaiah, who promises to redeem his servant and bring salvation to all nations, and the God of Hosea, who reclaims his wife, Gomer, who has become a prostitute, and loves her unconditionally as a parable of the love of God for Israel.

And quintessential, this is the God, Father Almighty, made known in the life, suffering, death, and resurrection of Jesus of Nazareth. Once again we are brought back to the fact that we rejoice to call God Father because Jesus did so and called us so to do.

In this light, the comments of John MacMurray in *Freedom in the Modern World* are very much to the point. MacMurray notes that most religions promise in one way or another to deliver their adherents from suffering. Such religions say to their devotees, "Follow me, and the things you fear will not happen to you." By contrast, says MacMurray, Christianity says, "Follow Christ, and some or all of the things that you fear may happen to you; *but you do not have to fear them anyway.*" Such confidence and courage are born from faith in God the Father Almighty who—even though we face the final enemy, death—will deliver us from the grave. We will consider this again in chapter 7 when we look at the resurrection of Jesus.

Bishop Woodie White serves United Methodists in Indiana. Some time ago he experienced one of the most difficult things he had ever faced in his life. He was sitting at home relaxing, watching his favorite team, the Washington Redskins, play. The phone rang and a relative exclaimed hysterically, "Woodie! Woodie! You had better come quick. Something terrible has happened to your mother. She has been raped!"

He immediately left Washington, D.C., for New York City. When he walked into his mother's house and saw her, she was frying chicken. Someone had broken into her home and robbed and raped her. Woodie stood immobile in a state of shock, but then he moved to his mother, took her tenderly in his arms, fighting back tears and anger.

As he was holding his mother, she said, "I'm frying chicken. I thought you might be hungry." And he was so overcome with the beauty of her spirit in the face of tragedy that he broke into tears.

Then his mother looked at him, and in her face was a wonderful light as she told her son, "Son, I want to tell you something, and I don't want you to ever forget it. Son, God is still good! God is good! God is good!"

God's almighty power is precisely this kind of love, this power of goodness and hope that this mother knew in her own soul and reflected even in the midst of her suffering and pain. This is the power and glory of the Father that Jesus portrayed in his story of the prodigal, and in all of his other stories and prayers. This is the power that Paul described in his praise of God's love in Christ from which nothing, absolutely nothing, can separate us (Romans 8). It is a power and a relationship that Christians have known throughout the ages. It is not a vengeful power or an arbitrary force. It does not leave us alone in our suffering. It travels with us through our pain, and it enables us to stand with courage exposing evil even when our own lives are at stake. It is the power of God's creative and redemptive love as shown to us in Jesus the Son—the power of the Father Almighty.

Summary

Jesus gave us our most powerful and descriptive image of God. We call God Father because we follow Jesus' example, so we understand this image in connection with Jesus. There is a sense in which we can assess how well one understands Christianity by how much one makes of the thought of being God's child, having God as Father.

The designation of God as Father has nothing to do with gender: God is not a sexual being. It describes a relationship of shared love and fellowship in which God pours out God's blessings on all God's children. God is our Creator and Liberator. Our relationship to God rescues us from sin and alienation and helps us remember who we are created to be. As God liberated the Jews from Egyptian bondage, so God rescues and redeems us from whatever bondage may enslave us.

God is all-powerful, almighty; but God's power is always defined, perhaps even limited, by God's love. Though we may not be delivered from pain and suffering, God is with us in our pain and suffering, sustaining us with almighty love. Even though we face the final enemy, death, God will deliver us from the grave, giving us eternal life.

CHAPTER TWO

JESUS CHRIST: GOD'S ONLY SON OUR LORD

Who is Jesus?

Nearly two thousand years ago, a child was born to Mary and to her husband, Joseph, a carpenter. The couple lived in an obscure Palestinian village, Nazareth, and the baby was born in Bethlehem. They named their baby boy Jesus.

Concerning Jesus' childhood, the New Testament writers record only one somewhat unusual incident. As was the custom among faithful Jewish parents, Mary and Joseph took Jesus to Jerusalem when he was twelve years old to be blessed in the Temple. On their return to Nazareth, about a day's journey from Jerusalem, they discovered that Jesus was not with them. They went back to Jerusalem and found him in the Temple, conversing with the elders. The accounts say that the elders were deeply impressed by his wisdom, and that Jesus already demonstrated an extraordinary sense of confidence in God as his Father.

This single event stands as the epitome for the New Testament writers of the events of Jesus' childhood and youth. They pick up the story again when Jesus was about thirty years old. At that time, a man named John the Baptist was baptizing people with water, symbolizing the forgiveness of sin. Jesus was baptized by John the Baptist and became a traveling preacher. That within itself was not an unusual thing; there were many itinerant preachers in that day. However, crowds began to follow him. They experienced something different about this preacher. They said things about him such as "no one ever spoke as this man is speaking." They experienced him as a person of gentle power and remarkable courage. Reports spread across the country that he was performing miracles, healing the sick and casting out demons.

Hardly three years passed before the religious leaders regarded Jesus as a threat and had him arrested. A weak Roman governor, more interested in participating in politics and keeping the peace than in doing justice to Jesus, imposed a death sentence on him. Jesus was crucified, a humiliating and agonizing death reserved for the lowest kind of criminal. His followers were terror stricken. They scattered, some of them denying that they had ever known him. Three days after his death, some of his followers experienced him *alive*. God had raised him from the dead and he appeared to his disciples.

Jesus could have been only a name in a footnote of a history book, quickly forgotten, but instead he became the best-known person ever to live on this earth. Twenty centuries after his ignominious death, men and women of every race and nationality in every corner of the globe revere him. His birth has become a pivotal moment in history to the point that the events of history are dated B.C. ("before Christ") and A.D. (*anno Domini*, "in the year of the Lord") on the calendar of Western civilization. Churches around the world display a cross, symbolizing the cross on which he died, as their symbol of faith and hope.

How do we account for this incredible intervention in human history? Who was this Jesus?

The Church has answered that question in a straightforward, albeit shocking manner. *Jesus is God's only Son, our Lord.* In other words, he is truly God and truly human—and these two dimensions of his nature are fully present in him. This is called the Incarnation; God has come to us in Jesus

Christ. (The meaning of the Incarnation is *enflesh*; that is, God is revealed in human flesh in Jesus.)

How could Jesus be human and divine?

How could Jesus be truly human and truly divine? That's the question we commonly ask, but really the question should not be *how* but *why*?

The Scandal of the Incarnation

Few men in the twentieth century seemed as immortal as Mao Tse-tung. Chairman Mao became the incarnation of a movement, a system of thought, and a revolution that affected 900,000 people. He lived to be eighty-three and was China's leader for over three decades. It was difficult for even the most astute observer to imagine a China without Chairman Mao. Yet he died. An admirer wrote, shortly after Mao's death: "He conceived of the Chinese Revolution, and then helped cause it to happen, and in the process, the thought of Chairman Mao became the primary thought of almost every Chinese. The word almost literally became flesh" (Schell, p. viii).

Note the conditional word: *almost*; "the word almost literally became flesh." The apostle John, writing of Jesus, said, "The Word became flesh." No reservation, no conditional definition. And Paul wrote, "The light of the knowledge of the glory of God [shines] in the face of Jesus Christ" (2 Corinthians 4:6).

I was in China two years after Mao's death. His likeness in picture and statue was everywhere. The little red book of his quotations was still in all the bookstores. Chairman Mao will take his place in history with great shapers of national life, but the limitation is still there. When I was in China, the magnificent mausoleum they had built for Chairman Mao was closed. The official word was that it was closed for repair, but the informal word passed on among the guides was that it was a deliberate effort to diminish Mao's presence in the minds and hearts of people; and that diminishing work goes on in China even today.

In Mao, powerful man that he was, the "word" of Chinese commitment and dogma *almost* became flesh. But with Jesus, the Word of God's creating and redeeming love became flesh and dwelt among us. We beheld his glory, "the glory as of the only begotten of the Father . . . full of grace and truth" (John 1:14 KJV). This is the *scandal of the Incarnation.* It is a scandal because it proclaims that in Jesus—the baby born in a barn, this poor preacher of Palestine—Christians praise and affirm as the ultimate revelation of God the key to the universe and all meaning.

The Wonder of the Incarnation

We misrepresent the Church's understanding of Christ if we oversimplify and define the Incarnation solely in terms of either Christ's divinity or his humanity. The Incarnation actually means that Jesus of Nazareth was a man, known by his disciples as being fully human, a person who shared the limitations and temptations of common, ordinary human existence—yet was also the deliberate and unique self-expression of God. P. T. Forsythe, a preacher-theologian, put it in a gripping way: "Our real and destined eternity goes round by Nazareth to reach us."

The first line in the Old Testament of the Bible is this: "In the beginning God created the heavens and the earth." The first line in John's Gospel of the New Testament is this: "In the beginning was the Word, and the Word was with God, and the Word was God." In the sentence from Genesis, the Source from which all comes is named. In the Gospel, John is making a decisive affirmation about who Jesus is. He is the expression of God's own true self. Consider Jesus' response to the question of Philip: "Lord, show us the Father." Jesus said to him, "Have I been with you all this time, Philip, and you still do not know me? Whoever has seen me has seen the Father " (John 14:9).

For the Greek term that John used at the beginning of his Gospel, our nearest English equivalent is *word*, but this by itself may not express fully what John had in mind. It was a term coined by Greek philosophers to suggest the creative, outgoing, self-revealing activity of God. And that's what John was trying to say. Christ was God and was with God in the beginning of all creation and now has come among us as God's self-revelation in human form. From these clear and intentionally vivid beginnings, Christians through the ages have always given praise to the Son as well as to the Father, and they have eschewed any concept or idea of a God that stands in contradiction to this.

This is Christianity's central and unique claim—the Incarnation: "And the Word became flesh and dwelt among us."

At the same time, the Christian claim is not only that Jesus reveals who God is and what God is like but also that he reveals who we are as human beings and what it means to become fully human. John says not only that "the Word was God" but also that "all things came into being through him" and that he was "the light of all people" (John 1:3-4). For Christian faith, Jesus is the key to human life in the world—the key to the life of God in the soul of human beings.

Why did Jesus come?

In his teachings, Jesus used parables to express profound truths. Louis Cassels wrote a modern parable about the Incarnation that helps us to grasp its meaning.

The story begins by describing a man who doesn't believe in the Incarnation and consequently thinks Christmas is "a lot of humbug." He is a nice man; he just doesn't understand the claim that God became man. One Christmas Eve his wife and children go to the midnight service, but he chooses to stay at home. Soon after they leave, it begins to snow, and he settles into a chair by the fire to read.

After several minutes pass, he is startled from his reading

by a thud at the window. There quickly follows another thud, then another. Thinking someone must be throwing snowballs at the window, he goes outside to investigate. What he sees is a flock of birds huddled in the snow. In an attempt to find shelter from the storm, they had tried to fly through his window.

He wonders how he can help the birds, and then he remembers the barn. It would make a good shelter. So he bundles up and heads to the barn. First he turns on a light, but the birds don't budge. Then he sprinkles a path of bread crumbs leading into the barn, but the birds do not notice. Finally he tries shooing them into the barn, but they scatter in every direction except the barn.

Cassels continues the story:

> "They find me a strange and terrifying creature," he said to himself, "and I can't seem to think of any way to let them know they can trust me.
>
> "If only I could be a bird myself for a few minutes, perhaps I could lead them to safety."
>
> Just at that moment, the church bells began to ring.
>
> He stood silently for a while, listening to the bells pealing the glad tidings of Christmas.
>
> Then he sank to his knees in the snow.
>
> "Now I do understand," he whispered. "Now I see why You had to do it." (Cassels, pp. 18-20)

Jesus Fulfills God's Promises

Does the coming of Jesus mean that Christians don't need the revelation of God in the Old Testament? The comparison we made above between Genesis 1 and John 1 shows that this cannot be true. Still, there is so much more to consider and enjoy about how Jesus fulfills God's promises and is God's defining expression of love and all he had sought to be and do even from the beginning of creation.

Covenant, as expressed in the Old and New Testaments, is the promise of God to fulfill God's vision of a people "loving God and loving their neighbors," in harmony not only with each other but also with creation. The Old Testament calls this state of relationship and being *shalom*. *Shalom* means "wholeness" or "completeness," and it applies to individuals and to society. If a person is in right relation to herself, to others, and to God, she will know shalom.

> I will make with them a covenant of [shalom]. . . . And they shall know that I am the LORD, when I break the bars of their yoke, and save them from the hands of those who enslaved them. They shall no more be plunder for the nations, nor shall the animals of the land devour them; they shall live in safety, and no one shall make them afraid. I will provide for them [plantations of shalom]. (Ezekiel 34:25, 27-29)

> > Then justice will dwell in the wilderness,
> >   and righteousness abide in the fruitful field.
> > The effect of righteousness will be [shalom],
> >   and the result of righteousness, quietness and trust
> >   forever. (Isaiah 32:16-17)

The effect of shalom also refers to our relationship to God's creation. This part of the vision of shalom is expressed by the prophet Isaiah:

> > The wolf shall live with the lamb,
> >   the leopard shall lie down with the kid,
> > the calf and the lion and the fatling together,
> >   and a little child shall lead them. (Isaiah 11:6)

The prophet goes on to say, "The earth will be full of the knowledge of the LORD / as the waters cover the sea" (Isaiah 11:9*b*).

For the ancient Hebrews, this vision of shalom—of peace, justice, and wholeness—was at the heart of all of God's purposes in history. All of God's creating and saving deeds on behalf of Israel had this vision in view. Along with the original purpose of creation, shalom was God's purpose in calling Abraham and Sarah so that their descendants would become a blessing to the whole world. And shalom was at the heart of the covenant with Moses at Sinai, where the law of God was given to guide the people in the way of love for God and neighbor. What is more, when the people failed to trust the God of creation and covenant, this same God sent the prophets with the same purpose in view—to turn the people from their sins, and to return them to the shalom of God.

The wonderful claim of the New Testament is that Jesus came to fulfill this ancient promise of shalom. He did this, according to the New Testament writers, by what he did, by who he was, and by what happened to him. In some passages, this sense of fulfillment comes as the answer to an ancient prediction, as when Matthew (2:5) recognizes the fulfillment of Micah's vision (5:2) in the birth of Jesus in the little town of Bethlehem. But much of the time the wonder of fulfillment springs from the fact that Jesus' followers recognized in him— in what he said and did—the restoration of the heart and soul of their own faith tradition. He went beneath the superficial and self-serving righteousness of the Pharisees to reclaim the weightier matters of the law—love for God and neighbor (Mark 12:28-34). He healed people, he fed them, and he was not ashamed to associate with poor or outcast persons or with sinners (Luke 7). Indeed, in all these things he embodied the same kind of tenacious love and justice that the ancients (Abraham, Isaac, Jacob, Joseph, Moses, David, Isaiah, and others) had always acclaimed of God; and he had to do this against the encrustations of legalism and intimidation that blinded the official leaders of religion in his day. Jesus fulfilled the Old Testament because he restored and embodied the promise of shalom in his life.

Covenant as Promise and Demand

The covenant was a promise; it was also a demand. "I will be your God, and you will be my people," God said to Abraham. And God gave Moses the Ten Commandments, the required imperatives of the love of God and the love of neighbor (Exodus 20:1-17). These are the precepts of shalom.

The people were free to be faithful or to violate the covenant. God's commitment to shalom is unwavering. God will not forsake his promise. As God does not choose to be God apart from the creation of the world, God does not choose to be God apart from covenant. Now covenant relationship requires freedom. So beginning with Adam and Eve, God gave us freedom. Adam and Eve exercised that freedom in disobedience. They ate the forbidden fruit, and thus the Bible tells the story of sin coming into the world, our separation from God.

From that point, the story of God's relationship to humankind is the story of covenant. The centerpiece of that covenant movement of God in early human history was the choosing of a particular people, the people of Israel, to bear God's light to all people. The Old Testament tells the story of the checkered career of that "people of God"—their faithfulness and disobedience.

So the Christian faith takes its understanding of God from the acts of God that begin with the Creation, are expressed vividly in covenant, but have their center in the coming of Jesus Christ. In the coming of Jesus, God came to us. Though we confess the mystery, the Christian view of reality is that the Jesus of history had his beginnings in eternity, and he is not separated from God and God's pursuit of his eternal purpose. To be sure, we are limited with words when we seek to talk about the mystery of the Incarnation.

I spent five years as a pastor in Gulfport, Mississippi. Though not an ardent fisherman, I fished enough to observe an interesting phenomenon that became a parable for Christ, "the image of the invisible God" as Paul calls him in Colossians 1.

Near the Bay of Biloxi in the Mississippi Sound, the level of the bayous changes with the high and low tides. These bayous feed the ocean, emptying their waters into the larger body at low tide. At high tide, the ocean feeds the bayous, raising their level. To the fisherman, there is significance other than the tide. Up the bayous for a certain distance, the water is brackish, flavored by the salt of the Gulf waters. White and speckled trout, whose natural habitat is the Gulf, are bountiful in this brackish water. But further inland, the waters lose their salt content, and freshwater fish such as green and rainbow trout hover in the cool depths.

The analogy is this: The bayous go to the ocean, but the ocean also comes to the bayous. Though limited, as all our words and parables are, it's a faint effort to picture Christ. Christ shows us what God is; he also shows us what all persons are meant to be. "Found in the fashion of man," he was human, revealing the model of our humanity—the image in which we were created. But also in him, the ocean of God has come to us. Christ is the image of God: a representation perfect enough to be a manifestation of God among us.

That's what John is saying in the beginning to his Gospel: "In the beginning was the Word, and the Word was with God, and the Word was God." Then John goes on to say, "In him was life, and the life was the light of all people. . . . And the Word became flesh and lived among us, and we have seen his glory, the glory as of a father's only son, full of grace and truth" (John 1:4, 14).

Believing in Jesus

If we take the record of the Old and New Testaments seriously, we will know that believing in God's goodness, trusting in God's promises, has never been easy or automatic for God's people. It was true for Israel, it was true for Jesus, and it has been true for the Church. The reason is not far to search out. In the midst of a fallen world—where glimpses of incredible beauty and hope are continually shattered by events of terrible tragedy and suffering—the decision to trust in God can seem like a weak alternative to a host of other methods whereby we struggle to *save ourselves.*

What must finally be grasped, however, is that there is a

great irony in the way God saves us. The "least has become greatest" (see Luke 9:48). The one with faith like a child (remember the boy Jesus in the Temple) becomes the model for all (Matthew 18:1-4). "The stone that the builders rejected has become the cornerstone" (see Acts 4:11). And all of this finds its quintessential moment of expression in the events of Jesus' crucifixion and resurrection. For there, as Paul says, Jesus did not try to save himself, but

> humbled himself
> and became obedient to death—
> even death on a cross!
> Therefore God exalted him to the highest place
> and gave him the name that is above every name,
> that at the name of Jesus every knee should bow, . . .
> and every tongue confess that Jesus Christ is Lord,
> to the glory of God the Father. (Philippians 2:8-11 NIV)

There is literally no limit to the depth and richness of God's promises as fulfilled in Jesus Christ. We might cite dozens of other references wherein the writers of the New Testament witness to their own amazement at finding the story of the Old Testament reembodied and brought to life in the story of Jesus. In subsequent chapters we shall see how the pattern of salvation given in Jesus is fulfilled yet again in the gift of the Holy Spirit and the way of salvation given to the world through Jesus' followers, the Church. Regardless of how many comparisons, connections, and illustrations we pile up, however, the wonder of the Incarnation cannot break through its scandal for us until we ourselves try the way of childlike faith. Only then, when we look to God our Father in and through Jesus, do we begin to understand truly why Christians throughout the ages have called him God's only Son, our Lord.

Summary

In the first chapter, I underscored the importance of images. The human mind needs to think visually. We need pictures. We may think and speak about the love of God, but without a specific image we end up saying that it is bound-less, infinite, beyond human telling, and so on, speaking abstractly or negatively in terms of what it is not. It is very difficult, I would say impossible, to begin with the universal when talking about God. To begin with the universal rather than the particular implies that we have knowledge of God independent of some other reality. That's the reason I made the case in chapter 1 that Christians cannot refer to or think about God as Father without connecting the image with Jesus, who made the image so powerfully real.

The Incarnation is essential to reveal in the flesh the God who has always been a God of love—a love that forgives, shows mercy, atones, and is trustworthy—a God already revealed in creation, covenant, law, and prophets, but now revealed in human flesh in Jesus. The revelation doesn't get any clearer than it is in Jesus, though it is the same revelation that has come in limited ways through other persons and from other places.

This is where *faith* comes in. The reality of God can be *proved*, but only to those who are open to the idea. That means that only you can prove God to yourself. Simply believing in God is not the issue. What kind of God do you believe in? This is why the Incarnation is so important. Our proof for believing in a loving, caring God who has kept and will keep covenant with us is our acceptance of Jesus Christ as Em-manuel—"God with us." Many logical arguments may be adequate for you to affirm that the existence of God is a reasonable probability. But that will not be enough, nor will it make much difference in your life. The only proof that will finally resolve your doubts and give meaning to your life is to experience God's reality for yourself.

CHAPTER THREE

SALVATION

What is sin?

Who Jesus is and why he came mean nothing to us unless we understand who we are and what our situation is in relation to God. The dominating plot of the human story from the Christian viewpoint has three movements that reflect good news, bad news, and good news: the Creation, the Fall, and redemption.

The Creation is good news. It is the work of grace. Out of freedom and love, God creates, and what God creates is good. Persons are created in God's image, and according to the Genesis account, God looks on all of creation and announces, "It is good."

Then comes the bad news movement in the plot, which disrupts God's intention and vision, mars the whole created order, and impairs our function and growth as humans. We call this bad news movement of the story the Fall.

I once saw a cartoon that captures the meaning of this dimension of human life. Brother Juniper, a character created by Father Justin Martyr, is a very humorous little monk who picks holes in the balloons of overly pious religious folks. He is at the zoo, looking into a cage where there is an ugly crowlike creature, a bird—bedraggled, scrimpy in feathering, a downcast-looking creature. The label on the cage says, "Bird of Paradise," and Brother Juniper comments, "I don't think he quite made it."

That's the bad news—and it's true of all of us. None of us "quite makes it." The possibilities of creation, God's vision and intention for us, are interrupted by our fall.

Estrangement from God

According to the Genesis account, it began with Adam and Eve in the garden. God's creation was good, and the crowns of his creation, Adam and Eve, are placed in that garden of creation with everything perfect. Only one thing is prohibited: They are not to eat of the forbidden fruit. They do precisely what God commands them not to do, and they are driven from the garden. They are now estranged from God and spend the rest of their lives east of Eden, outside the wonderful relationship God intended.

Adam's story is our story. After all, his name means "humankind." So, we don't need to be preoccupied with *how* it happened—how sin came into the world. *That* it happened and *what* is the result are altogether too obvious. God's vision of peace and harmony in creation has been disfigured. The image of God within each of us has been distorted. We all know a deep sense of separation from God. Things just aren't right. We don't know peace. Something is lacking in the realization of our potential for wholeness.

We call it *sin*. However we look at it and name it, the result is a condition that is universally human, a dramatic alteration of our created relationship with God. This condition leaves us flawed, fallible, and off center, in other words, unable to live in right relationship with God. Try as we might, we are unable by our own power to act righteously, to act in harmony with God. Paul describes the person under conviction and how the recognition of God's love in Christ can free us: "I do not do the good I want, but the evil I do not want is what I do. . . . Wretched man that I am! Who will rescue me from this body of death?" (Romans 7:19, 24). We all know the feeling, don't we?

The condition of sin permeates our entire beings. Perhaps its most dreadful consequence is that it estranges us from God. Our highest destiny is to know God, to live in personal relationship and harmony with God. Sin makes that relationship impossible. The prophet Isaiah gave expression to it:

> See, the LORD's hand is not too short to save,
>   nor his ear too dull to hear.
> Rather, your iniquities have been barriers
>   between you and your God,
> and your sins have hidden his face from you.
> (Isaiah 59:1-2)

Is it not this estrangement from God that accounts for our restlessness? We have a hunger deep within our hearts that only God can satisfy. There is a vacuum in our souls that only God can fill. It's who we are, created in the image of God, but missing the destiny for which God made us.

Enslavement to Self

But we are also enslaved. Sin alienates us from God, and it brings us into captivity. Again, Paul gives dramatic expression to it: I am "sold into slavery under sin. I do not understand my own actions. For I do not do what I want, but I do the very thing I hate. . . . In fact, it is no longer I that do it, but sin that dwells within me" (Romans 7:14-15, 17).

This is the reason we are oppressed by the seeming permanence of our separation from God and our powerlessness to heal ourselves and live as in our heart of hearts we would like to live. Our wills are weak. We want to live as God would have us live, but we seem impotent. We don't seem to have the power to act in harmony with God; in fact, we are slaves to our distorted ideas, addictions, and longings and to the pervasive pull of sin in our lives.

Separation from Others

Sin brings estrangement from God and enslavement to self, and it separates us—puts us in conflict with others. Is it hard to see? When we look seriously at our relationships, if we are willing to even consider the fact of sin, it doesn't take long to realize that sin is the root problem. We are separated from God and therefore not fulfilling our potential as persons in God's image. We are enslaved by our own sinful selves, our selfishness, greed, and distorted notion of security and meaning. The overflow of that puts us in conflict with others.

Let me focus this in a concrete way. As an ordained minister for over thirty years, I have seen only a few divorces between husbands and wives the cause of which could not be readily identified as sin. More often than not, it was sin expressing itself as self-centeredness, pride, perverted sexual passion, or distorted security needs. The common causes for divorce are labeled as (1) breakdown of communication, (2) loss of shared goals and interests, (3) sexual incompatibility, and (4) infidelity. Look at those cause labels. Do they not all reflect interpersonal conflict? And most interpersonal conflict is rooted in self-centeredness, pride, and uncontrolled passion or greed. Just as sin brings estrangement from God and enslavement to our selves—our distorted ideas, addictions, and longings—it breaks human love relationships.

Scripture talks about the mystery of iniquity. A mystery enshrouds sin and sin's power in our lives. For that reason, again, we should not be preoccupied with how it happened or happens. But it's a life-and-death matter to realize *that* it happens and what it does to us. It estranges us from God, it enslaves us to self, and it puts us in conflict with others. Our predicament is that we are powerless to do anything about it. Bad news!

Good news, bad news, and now the third movement in the plot of the human story—the good news of redemption through Jesus Christ.

What is salvation?

Among Christians in Africa, the New Testament word for redemption means "God took our heads out." It's a rather awkward phrase, but when you trace it back to the nineteenth century when slave trading was practiced, the meaning becomes powerful. White men invaded African villages and carried men, women, and children off into slavery. Each slave had an iron collar buckled around his or her neck, and the collar was attached to a chain. The chained slaves would be driven to the coastline and shipped to England and the United States.

From time to time, as the chain of slaves would make their way to the coast, a relative, a loved one, or a friend would recognize someone who had been captured as a slave and would offer a ransom for the captors to remove the collar and free the person. Thus the word for redemption: "God took our heads out."

However we state it, whatever image we use out of our own tradition, the word *redemption* means God's action to set us free from the bondage of sin, guilt, and death.

Continuing to think about redemption in the context of slavery, the ransom theme was vividly seen in Abraham Lincoln's Emancipation Proclamation: "That on the first day of January, in the year of our Lord one thousand eight hundred and sixty-three, all persons held as slaves within any State, or designated part of a State, the people whereof shall then be in rebellion against the United States, shall be then, thenceforward, and forever free." It is little wonder that when Abraham Lincoln died, thousands of people lined the railroad tracks as the body of the president was taken from Washington to Illinois for burial.

In some cities along the way there were special ceremonies. There is one story, perhaps without sources to support its authenticity, that bears great truth. In one of the cities where the casket of the dead president was carried in a processional through the streets, an African American woman stood on the curb and lifted her little boy as high as she could above the heads of the crowd. As she held him there so that he could see, she was overheard to say, "Take a long look, honey. He died for you."

In the last chapter we talked about the person of Jesus Christ, the Incarnation—God coming to us as a human being. Now we focus on the primary purpose of his coming: the salvation of humankind.

One statement in the Apostles' Creed affirms, "I believe . . . in Jesus Christ . . . [who] was crucified." In the Christian view of reality, there is no complete and saving knowledge of God apart from the cross of Jesus Christ. No Christian theology is complete without the Cross. Every point of Christian theological affirmation is understood in light of the Cross. There is a real sense in which we can say that the purpose of the coming of Christ was the Cross. The Cross was the climax of God's saving action.

Countless hymns of the Church pick up this theme. One of the most glorious expressions of it is a hymn by Charles Wesley, "O For a Thousand Tongues to Sing":

> He breaks the power of canceled sin,
> he sets the prisoner free;
> his blood can make the foulest clean;
> his blood availed for me.

We need to note again that it is not the death of Christ on the cross alone that provides our salvation. All Christ was and did, which climaxes with the Cross and includes the Resurrection, the Ascension (forty days after the Resurrection, Jesus left earth and entered heaven), and the coming of the Holy Spirit, is God's saving work.

In one of the most familiar words of Scripture, John 3:16, it is stated, "For God so loved the world that he gave his only Son, so that everyone who believes in him may not perish but have eternal life." This is what Paul argued so convincingly about in his Letter to the Romans: "Since all have sinned and fall short of the glory of God; they are now justified by his grace as a gift, through the redemption that is in Christ Jesus, whom God put forward as a sacrifice of atonement by his blood, effective through faith" (Romans 3:23-25). And in the First Epistle of John, there is this sentence: "And we have seen and do testify that the Father has sent his Son as the Savior of the world" (4:14).

The New Testament is full of passages like these that bring together the person and the work of Jesus Christ. Jesus is the divine Son of God who came to be our Savior. His undeserved death on the cross is the center of the Incarnation. In other words, the Incarnation is not just a *means* to his passion and death. Rather, the Incarnation is itself an expression of the same love that led to the Cross (see Philippians 2).

Jesus did this saving work by living among us, teaching, healing, dying on a cross, and rising again from the dead. So, the salvation work of Jesus Christ is justification, reconciliation, and liberation. (*Justification* is the process by which we are made right with God through God's grace. *Reconciliation* means being brought back into relationship with God through the death of Jesus on the cross. *Liberation* is deliverance from sin.) These are not separate movements of God's salvation in Jesus Christ but different ways of talking about the salvation experience.

Salvation as Justification

Justification by grace through faith is a pivotal truth of the Christian faith. It is the answer to the question, How can sinners be put right with God? How can our estrangement from God be dissolved?

I remember going to court with a young man. I was there to offer my personal and pastoral support. It was a trial before a judge, not before a jury. The prosecuting attorney and then the defense attorney made their cases before the judge. Written testimonies and other evidence had already been given to the judge. After the arguments, the judge invited the young man to stand before the bar of the court. She began to speak. It was a kind of lecture. The more she spoke, the more I thought to myself, *This is it; he's going to end up in jail.*

I was surprised as the judge came to her conclusion: "This court finds you not guilty." I sighed deeply as I saw a look of tremendous release come over the face of the young man. But then came the challenging word from the judge: "Young man, because the court finds you not guilty does not mean that you are innocent."

I knew, as did the young man, that there was not enough evidence to convict him of what he was accused in that court of law, but indeed, he was not innocent.

That's a hint, however faint, of the meaning of justification by grace through faith. We are all guilty. As Paul said, "We have all sinned and fallen short of the glory of God—there is none righteous, no, not one" (see Romans 3:23, 10). And we all know that—how well we know our sin! But God has shown and reaffirmed his great love for us by giving us Jesus Christ as a sacrifice, as a substitute, as a power over sin. His death on the cross was death on our behalf. When we receive that sacrificial love by faith, we are justified; that is, we are made right with God.

As already indicated, justification is a metaphor from the law courts, so when we talk about salvation as justification, the imagery is that of being on trial before God. The Greek word translated "to justify" means not to *make* someone something but to *treat,* to *reckon,* or to *account* someone as something. This is the picture: When we appear before God, we are anything but innocent. We have sinned; we are estranged; we have broken the relationship; we are utterly guilty. Yet, God *treats us, reckons us, accounts us* as if we were innocent. That is what justification means.

In the Christian view of reality, we talk about justification by grace through faith. Through our faith in Jesus Christ, and what God has done for us in Jesus Christ, we are justified. It is all a matter of grace—God's grace—God's gift of love and full acceptance of us.

Salvation as Reconciliation

The Cross is the ultimate expression of God's love. It is a vivid picture of God's nature. It came home to me in a poster that moved me to tears. The words on the poster were these: "Do you want to know how much God loves you?" Jesus answered, "This much!" The picture on the poster was Jesus, his arms outstretched and nailed to a cross. So, Jesus spreads out his arms on the cross and says to each one of us, "This is how much I love you."

Reconciliation is another way of talking about salvation. It is really very much like justification. A pivotal passage in the salvation story is 2 Corinthians 5:

> From now on, therefore, we regard no one from a human point of view; even though we once knew Christ from a human point of view, we know him no longer in that way. So if anyone is in Christ, there is a new creation: everything old has passed away; see, everything has become new. All this is from God, who reconciled us to himself through Christ, and has given us the ministry of reconciliation; that is, in Christ God was reconciling the world to himself, not counting their trespasses against them, and entrusting the message of reconciliation to us. (Vv. 16-19)

Our sinful condition is that we are separated from God, but because of Jesus Christ, God does not count our trespasses against us. That's justification. We are reconciled to God by the loving death of Jesus Christ. The Cross is a pledge of God's total acceptance in the face of sin's total destructiveness. In chapter 1, we talked about God as our Father and how God has adopted us. Michael Green has put that truth in a gripping sentence: The Cross "is the adoption certificate into the family, the naturalization papers into the kingdom" (Green, p. 74).

Think for a moment about the dynamic of this reconciling love. Modern psychology has shown that only he who is loved can allow himself to be loved and can himself love: "Only the beloved can be a lover." It is knowing that God loves us that allows us to love him. It's also knowing that we are loved by God that we are able to love ourselves and love our neighbors. The Gospel writer, John, captured it in this way: "We love because first he loved us" (1 John 4:19). The surest sign, even a test, of whether we have experienced the totally accepting love of Jesus Christ is the extent to which we reenact that love.

Salvation as Liberation

Justification speaks of becoming aware of the enormity of God's love. Reconciliation speaks of estranged friends being brought back into relationship. The third way we speak of salvation—liberation—speaks of being delivered from bondage, saved from the control and oppression of an enemy. The primary language of the early church for this particular movement was restoration, the restoration or re-creation of the image of God in human life and relationships. So, we cannot speak of salvation without speaking of liberation from the tyranny of sin, evil, and death.

The Christian story is the story of liberation. The Bible witnesses to it over and over. The deliverance of the people of Israel out of Egyptian bondage is in the context of God speaking: "I have seen my people in bondage and I have come to deliver them." That's the story of Exodus in the Old Testament that parallels the ministry of Christ in the New

Testament. In the Gospel of Mark, Jesus comes on the stage as the Great Deliverer, liberating people from every form of bondage—calling people to repent, healing people, and casting out demons.

In Luke's Gospel, Jesus launches his public ministry in the synagogue of his hometown, Nazareth, by reading from the prophet Isaiah:

> The Spirit of the Lord is upon me,
>   because he has anointed me to bring good news to the poor.
> He has sent me to proclaim release to the captives
>   and recovery of sight to the blind,
>   to let the oppressed go free,
> to proclaim the year of the Lord's favor. (Luke 4:18-19)

When he finished that reading, as the eyes of all were focused upon him, he said, "Today this scripture has been fulfilled in your hearing."

Near the end of his life, Jesus gave a parable of the last judgment. In that parable he talked about people being separated according to what they had done—some would go to the right, some to the left. Those to the right would receive the eternal reward of heaven; those to the left would be cast into outer darkness. The basis on which the judgment rested was how people had responded to the least of these: hungry, naked, widowed, imprisoned, and sick persons. Jesus even said that people who were agents of liberation to "the least of these," engaged in ministry to hungry and oppressed persons, but who did not yet know and confess his name, nevertheless were suffering with him on behalf of the ones whom he had come to "seek and to save." As a result of participating in that kind of liberating ministry, they were sharing in Christ's saving work, deliverance from the powers of bondage and estrangement. (See Matthew 25:31-46.)

There would be others who confessed his name yet failed to follow him on the road to a ministry of liberation; others who failed to be as Christ to estranged, helpless, oppressed, and marginalized persons. Though they confessed they knew Christ, they would be judged as those who didn't know him. The bottom line was very clear: Knowing him means experiencing him as the liberator and following him by sharing the liberating and reconciling grace with others.

The Liberator is present wherever evil is confronted and wherever the bread of freedom is won. But he is also present when that victory is not yet won, where people continue to suffer and are victimized, oppressed, cold, hungry, or homeless. He is present there as the One who has been there himself, even knowing the abandonment of the Father when he hung on the cross and cried in anguish, "My God, my God, why hast thou forsaken me?"

The work of salvation is the work of liberation, and Christ is liberating today as he liberated in his days of the flesh— using the same weapon of suffering love with which he defeated the enemies that beset his world.

My wife, Jerry, is involved as a volunteer in a ministry to people who are in jail. One dimension of ministry is advocacy—being an advocate for those who are imprisoned, who for the most part have been forgotten, and who have become the victims of a calloused system that is completely inadequate and far more committed to punishment than to reconciliation and restitution. Every week she comes home with stories that tear at my heart and threaten to drive me to despair, because we seem to be helpless in the presence of such a harvest of oppression and estrangement.

She has found in jail

- a mentally ill person, pregnant with her fourth child, diagnosed with AIDS, who needed to be in a hospital rather than behind bars.
- a street person with no place to live who was found sitting in a swing in someone's yard and was arrested for trespassing.
- a woman who wandered away from her care-home, got hungry, robbed a bank, bought hamburgers and some

houseshoes, boarded a bus back to the bank she robbed, and returned the unused money.

Jerry has discovered the truth that the gospel word to us is that Christ as our contemporary is to be found as the liberator, often incognito, wherever hungry persons are being fed, naked persons clothed, and prisoners attended to. Jesus said, "As you did it to one of the least of these . . . , you did it to me" (Matthew 25:40).

It is no surprise that a whole system called liberation theology has developed in our time because of the heightened awareness of systemic evil. One of the pivotal claims of liberation theology, which is a central witness of the Bible, is that God has taken a preferential option on behalf of people who are poor.

In the Christian understanding of salvation, liberation must come as deliverance for all those who are disenfranchised and oppressed. It must come as empowerment to older as well as younger persons, male as well as female, every minority group, disabled as well as dispossessed persons. Salvation's work is taking place wherever the shackles of human bondage are being torn off and oppressed persons are being set free.

The enemies of God are sin, evil, and death. The saving work of Jesus Christ, which fulfills the ministry of the Old Testament prophets, is deliverance from those foes.

Did Jesus suffer and die for *me*?

One of the great difficulties in thinking about the meaning of the Cross is understanding how the death of Christ can have anything to do with *me*. How can this be a solution to my sin, to my estrangement from God? Whatever we believe about the fall of Adam and Eve, when we are clear in our thinking, we must admit that from the very beginning of human history, persons have chosen to go their own way. We have been rebels against God's design, hostile and self-centered, thus experiencing all the misery that such rebellion, hostility, and self-centeredness bring. It's futile to deny this. Someone has put it sharply: "The heart of our problems is the problem of our hearts."

The question is, What can God do about it? God could control us completely, force us into relationship. But that would be in total violation of our free will—the free will that he has given us to choose. It would also be in violation of his love and his willingness to allow us to love as an invested choice, not just an involuntary reflex.

God could go the opposite way and condemn us permanently to separation and estrangement from him. And who could argue with the fairness of that?

If there were no morality involved or a sense of fairness and equity, if there were no values or issues that truly affect the quality of life, God could pretend that what we do does not matter, that our sin and wickedness are okay in the drama of human life and in God's relationship to us. But what would that say about God's integrity and justice? What would that say about a differentiation between right and wrong?

God's bold dream of salvation with justice was acted out on the cross. There we see complete fairness, unquestionable justice, extravagant love, and breathtaking generosity. On the cross, God took our place! That's the gospel. Through the Cross, God condemned the sin and wickedness of human beings and took the punishment for that sin into his own person.

> He faced up to the poison in human hearts and drank the bitter cup of death Himself. He did not pretend that our debts to Him were not astronomical. But He paid for them out of His own account, and it crushed Him. . . .
>
> Some people present it as a cold transaction, as if God the Father punished Jesus in our place. Often they back it up with legal analogies, which are less than just and less than helpful—as if a judge would cause (or even allow) the wrong person to be

punished. That is not God's way. What He did was absolutely just and fair. It was the solution that gave complete satisfaction both to His holiness and to His love. He upheld the penalty we deserved—and then went and endured it Himself. And because Jesus was *human,* it was a person standing for the human race at the place of our greatest need. Because Jesus was *God* as well as man, the effect of what He has done is limitless. It explains how God could accept people like Abraham and David in Old Testament days who knew nothing of Christ but were clearly reveling in divine forgiveness. They were forgiven because of what Jesus was going to do on the cross. It explains how God can accept us, so many centuries later, because of what Jesus did, once and for all, on the cross. It explains how God may well be able to welcome people who genuinely seek Him but have no knowledge of Him because of their historical or religious circumstances. (Green, pp. 73-74)

As the writer of the First Epistle of John puts it, Jesus "is the atoning sacrifice for our sins, and not for ours only but also for the sins of the whole world" (1 John 2:2).

Our sins separated us from God, so Christ, God's Son, died to remove the barrier and take care of the sin problem. Theologians call this the Atonement. Many theories have been devised to explain this atoning work of Christ. Twentieth-century theologians express their understanding in different ways. Karl Barth believes not that Christ suffered punishment in order to satisfy the wrath of God but that he is the Judge being judged in our place. God does not *represent* us but *replaces* us.

Emil Brunner contends that the Atonement begins with a serious view of sin and guilt, along with the fact that Christ suffered on our behalf, his death being the penalty for our sin.

Reinhold Niebuhr maintains that the mystery of the Atonement cannot be understood, but what we know is that God takes our sinfulness into himself and suffers for us so that justice and forgiveness may be experienced.

Not one of these persons or any specific theory of the

Atonement—in fact, not all of them put together—can fathom the mystery and make clear why the Cross is our salvation. What we *do* know and what we affirm is not the Cross alone but the whole life of Jesus is God's redeeming act.

The famous plastic surgeon Dr. Maxwell Maltz, who wrote the best-selling book *Psycho-Cybernetics,* tells a story that gives us a shadowy glimpse of the mystery and meaning of the Cross for our salvation.

A woman came to see Dr. Maltz one day about her husband. She told the doctor that her husband had been injured in a fire while attempting to save his parents from a burning house. He couldn't get to them. They both were killed, and his face was burned and disfigured. He had given up on life and gone into hiding. He wouldn't let anyone see him—not even his wife.

Dr. Maltz told the woman not to worry. "With the great advances we've made in plastic surgery in recent years," he said, "I can restore his face."

She explained that he wouldn't let anyone help him because he believed God disfigured his face to punish him for not saving his parents.

Then she made a shocking request: "I want you to disfigure my face so I can be like him! If I can share in his pain, then maybe he will let me back into his life. I love him so much, I want to be with him. And if that is what it takes, then that is what I want to do."

Of course, Dr. Maltz would not agree, but he was moved deeply by that wife's determined and total love. He got her permission to try to talk to her husband. He went to the man's room and knocked, but there was no answer. He called loudly through the door, "I know you are in there and I know you can hear me, so I've come to tell you that my name is Dr. Maxwell Maltz. I'm a plastic surgeon, and I want you to know that I can restore your face."

There was no response. Again he called loudly, "Please come out and let me help restore your face." But again there was no answer. Still speaking through the door, Dr. Maltz told the man what his wife was asking him to do. "She wants me to disfigure her face, to make her face like yours in the hope that you will let her back into your life. That's how much she loves you. That's how much she wants to help you!"

There was a brief moment of silence, and then ever so slowly, the doorknob began to turn. The disfigured man came out to make a new beginning and to find a new life. He was set free, brought out of hiding, given a new start by his wife's love.

It's a dramatic expression of human love that gives us a picture, however faint, of the saving love of Jesus Christ, what we call the Atonement.

How do I receive salvation?

The question then becomes, What must we do to receive the gracious love and forgiveness of God?

First of all, we must see ourselves as we are and realize our need. A big part of this is the realization that we have sinned, and that our sin is separating us from God, from our best selves, and from others.

With an awareness, then, that God is a loving Father who hurts because we are separated from him and that our sins are offenses against him, we are sorry, deeply sorry. We repent—that is, we turn around; we decide to return to the Father and accept the grace that he offers.

That grace is accepted by faith, faith that Jesus is indeed our Savior; that is God's gift of love to us for our justification, reconciliation, and liberation. We receive the gift, and it is that: Our salvation is a gift; we receive it in faith.

Summary

Christ came into the world to show us what God is like and teach us what God expects. Yet, there was more. His mission on earth culminated in his death on the cross. Jesus crowned his ministry with the sacrifice of his own life.

For what purpose? Why would Jesus do that? The earliest Christians answered, "Christ also suffered for [our] sins once and for all, the righteous for the unrighteous, in order to bring [us] to God" (1 Peter 3:18; see also 1 Corinthians 15:3).

The death of Jesus on the cross was unlike any other death because of who Jesus was. As we considered earlier, God was in Christ. Jesus embodied the fullness of God in a human being. So we talk about the two natures of Jesus—divine and human. Though that is a staggering claim, there is no other satisfactory explanation of who Jesus is.

We look at the cross not in terms of just any death. We look at it in the light of who died on the cross. Here is the extreme example of love. Jesus went to the cross voluntarily for our sakes. In the images of the New Testament, he was the Good Shepherd who laid down his life for the sheep. On one occasion he said, "No one has greater love than this, to lay down one's life for one's friends" (John 15:13).

Jesus went beyond that. He was not laying down his life only for his friends. He was laying down his life for people who had never heard of him, people who were apathetic, even hostile, toward God and all that God sought to do. That is what the apostle Paul is dealing with when he contemplates the wonder of the love of Jesus on the cross: "Christ died for the ungodly. Indeed, rarely will anyone die for a righteous person—though perhaps for a good person someone might actually dare to die. But God proves his love for us in that while we still were sinners Christ died for us" (Romans 5:6-8).

As I was working on this chapter, I discovered a revealing fact about Christ. In Scripture and in Christian worship, he is *named* for our every need. To hungry persons, he is the Bread of Life; to thirsty persons, he is the Fountain of Living Water; to lonely persons, he is the Friend who is willing to go the second mile and make the ultimate sacrifice; to sick persons, he is the Balm in Gilead; to dying persons, he is the Resurrection and the Life. The naming reaches its pinnacle on the cross where Isaiah's prophecy of the coming Messiah is realized: There he was "numbered with the transgressors" (Isaiah 53:12). The Cross is the ultimate expression of God's love.

Our sin separates us from God. Jesus Christ, God's Son, died to remove the barrier and to take care of our sin problem. As the forgiving love of God, Christ provides salvation—justification, reconciliation, and liberation. We do not deserve this salvation. No religious observances or good deeds could ever earn it. Christianity is not a system of merit. God's salvation—his love, forgiveness, and acceptance—is all gift. Christ died to save us because we cannot save ourselves. We receive this gracious gift of salvation by faith.

CHAPTER FOUR

THE HOLY SPIRIT

What is the Trinity?

In the musical *The Song of Bernadette,* there is a line that suggests, "Those who believe need no explanation; for those who do not believe, no explanation will satisfy."

Perhaps the most debatable Christian doctrine is what we call the Trinity. The early Christians felt they could not explain their experience of God without talking about God *the Father,* God *the Son,* and God *the Holy Spirit.* In chapters 1 and 2 we explored the first two persons of the Trinity, God the Father and God the Son, but I have waited until now to define the Trinity because it is now that we are ready to discuss the third person of the Trinity, the Holy Spirit.

As is true at so many points of Christian doctrine, there is mystery in the Trinity. When we talk about the Trinity, we do not mean that we believe in three Gods. We believe *not* in a trinity of Gods but in a *triune* God—one God who exists and manifests himself in three different persons. We might express it thus: "God everywhere, God there, and God here," or "God for us, God with us, and God in us."

Compared to the first disciples, we are at a disadvantage because we do not have the chance of listening to Jesus personally as a physically present being. On the other hand, we are at a great advantage because of his promise of the Holy Spirit, his own unseen self, being available to us. While he lived on earth, the Holy Spirit's acts and words were concentrated within Jesus. With his death and resurrection, Christ's presence was available to all who would receive him.

The doctrine of the Trinity is the report by Christians of their experience in relation to God. Robert McAfee Brown, an ordained minister, religious educator, and writer, imagines a discussion held in the adult study hour of the First Church at Ephesus. The topic was "Who is the God we worship?"

> First Answer: We worship the God of our fathers (and mothers), the God of Abraham, Isaac, and Jacob (and Sarah, Leah, and Rachel), who has always been and always will be.
>
> Second Answer: Amen to all that, with the addition that it is this very same God who has drawn near to us, entered into and shared our lot in Jesus of Nazareth; to enact, rather than just talk about, God's love for us. This is one reason we have kept the Hebrew scriptures as part of our own sacred writings, so that nobody will miss the connection.
>
> Third Answer: Amen once again to both those claims, with the addition that it is this same God-of-our-Ancestors-Also-Revealed-in-Jesus-of-Nazareth whose presence we feel *here and now*, day after day, and especially when we gather to break bread and share wine. The breath of God, God's Spirit, empowers us and makes God our contemporary.
>
> Program Chairman: Anybody taking notes. Let's get it written down. One God (not three) in three manifestations (not two or five). (Brown, p. 164)

If I had been the program chairman in the church of Ephesus, I would not have used the word *manifestations*. I would have said *persons*. There are many manifestations of God but three persons. I would have said three persons because I am the recipient of the results of the Church struggling with attempts to understand and define God. For a long time the Church groped for a way to formulate intellectually and conceptually its faith in God as Father, Jesus Christ, and the

Holy Spirit. What the New Testament writers witness to cried out for elaboration and clarification, yet they were convinced that this God had revealed himself in a threefold way as Father, Son, and Holy Spirit. Not until the Council of Nicaea in A.D. 325 (the first ecumenical council of the church) was the notion of the triune nature of God established in a creed and recognized as the doctrine of the Church. The Nicene Creed affirms

> We believe in one God,
>   the Father, the Almighty . . .
>
> We believe in one Lord, Jesus Christ,
>   the only Son of God . . .
>
> We believe in the Holy Spirit, the Lord, the giver of life,
>   who proceeds from the Father and the Son,
>   who with the Father and the Son
>   is worshiped and glorified . . .

So when we talk about the Trinity, we are talking about God the Father Almighty, God who became human in Jesus Christ, and God who is present with us now as the Holy Spirit.

In chapter 2, we mentioned the fact that the Jesus of history had his beginnings in eternity. Christ was God and was with God in the beginning of all creation. The same is true of the Holy Spirit. So we are talking not about three Gods but about a triune God—God in three persons. C. S. Lewis offered a model for explaining the essence of the Trinity by reflecting on the expression "God is love."

> All sorts of people are fond of repeating the Christian statement that "God is love." But they seem not to notice that the words "God is love" have no real meaning unless God consists of at least two Persons. Love is something that one person has for another person. If God was a single person, then before the world was made, He was not love. (Lewis, pp. 135-36)

When a Christian says, "God is love," she does not mean what many people mean. She is not saying "love is God." Instead, the meaning is that within the very essence of God is a vital, living, dynamic relationship of love that has been going on within God forever. This immanent relationship of love existed before the Creation; and in fact, it is only because of this complete and self-giving relationship of love between the Father and the Son that the world was made.

The Father loves the Son (John 5:20), and the Son loves the Father (John 14:31). Out of this relationship of perfect love is generated a Spirit of divine love, who is the personal Spirit of the Father and the Son as they love each other. Lewis illustrated this generation and procession of the person of Spirit by comparing it to the generation of a "spirit" by any communal relationship among human beings. A winning football team has a certain spirit; a losing football team has a different spirit. A young couple recently married reveals a certain spirit, while a young couple facing divorce reveals another spirit. All such spirits are not alike; but every family, club, or team has a spirit and communicates that spirit to those outside the communal relationship as well as to those inside.

> We talk of this as the spirit not of each individual member but of the group as a whole because the individual members, when they are together, do really develop particular ways of talking and behaving which they would not have if they were apart. It is as if a sort of communal personality came into existence. Of course, it is not a real person: it is only rather like a person. But that is just one of the differences between God and us. What grows out of the joint life of the Father and the Son is a real Person, is in fact the Third of the three Persons who are God. (Lewis, p. 136)

To be sure, there is a mystery here, and we will never probe the depths of that mystery. However, since we are called to love God with our minds, as well as with heart, soul, and strength, we continue to reflect on our faith and seek to give expression to it. Though we try to give expression to what we believe, the core issue is that we don't experience relationship with a belief statement; our relationship is with the God of whom the belief statement speaks. Upon reflection, most of us would testify to having experienced God in the ways that the people of that imagined church conference in Ephesus did. Therefore, from that time until now, reports on the experience of God in this fashion have been a part of our lives.

We certainly do not have to experience the three persons of the Trinity in a particular order. Persons who know little about the faith or those who are just coming to the faith may talk more about experiencing the reality of the Spirit of God in their lives before they begin to formulate any understanding of the God who is "the Father Almighty, maker of heaven and earth." And in all probability, they would have that reality of the Spirit of God in their lives reinforced by the story of Jesus. Those two clues lead them to confirm a belief in God who creates and is sovereign over all.

Others may not begin with the Spirit. That may be too vague and undefined for them. They may begin with Jesus, in whom they have begun to experience a compassion, a love, and a life-style that completely grab their imagination and eventually their commitment. Only then do they begin to understand that this human Jesus is as much of God as could ever be contained in human form, and they are able to move to understanding and experiencing Jesus Christ as God's expression in "a person like as we are." So the Incarnation becomes the first part of their experience.

These persons who begin with Jesus, as they seek to learn more about him, as they make commitments to follow him, discover the need to be empowered by something beyond themselves. As the presence of Christ grows real in their lives, they begin to think of Christ with them, and so the Holy Spirit becomes a reality.

Who is the Holy Spirit?

The Holy Spirit is God himself at work in human life. God as Spirit was working in the world long before Christ came, but the coming of Christ revealed even more clearly the character of God's Spirit. And the New Testament affirms that the Spirit came in a special way after the resurrection and ascension of Jesus. On the Day of Pentecost, fifty days after the Resurrection, a small company of those first-century Christians became aware of a new empowering presence in their lives that would make the truth of the gospel real to them, inspire them in mission, and energize them in doing God's will.

Jesus promised them the Spirit before he was crucified. He said, "I will ask the Father, and he will give you another Advocate, to be with you forever. This is the Spirit of truth, whom the world cannot receive, because it neither sees him nor knows him. You know him, because he abides with you, and he will be in you" (John 14:16-17). Then he said the same thing in a more picturesque way: "I will not leave you orphaned; I am coming to you. In a little while the world will no longer see me, but you will see me; because I live, you also will live" (Vv. 18-19). He summarized his teaching about the Spirit in John's Gospel with these words: "I have said these things to you while I am still with you. But the Advocate, the Holy Spirit, whom the Father will send in my name, will teach you everything, and remind you of all that I have said to you" (Vv. 25-26).

So the Holy Spirit was given in an explicit way after the crucifixion and resurrection of Jesus, not to be a substitute for Christ's absence, but really to accomplish forever Christ's presence. The Holy Spirit is Christ alive, indwelling us. Someone has given it a cryptic description: The Holy Spirit is "the life of God in the soul of man."

What does the Holy Spirit do?

In the Hebrew language of the Old Testament and the Greek of the New Testament, the words for "wind," "breath," and "spirit" are the same. The association of these three words can help us understand the richness of the biblical witness to the person and work of the Holy Spirit.

The Holy Spirit Brings Life

In the Gospel of John, there is a story of a Pharisee named Nicodemus, a leader of the Jews, who came to Jesus by night seeking to know more about this man Jesus—the transforming power that was flowing from his life, the fact that he was claiming so many disciples, and the reality that he was bringing something new and different and dynamic to the faith. He acknowledged his appreciation for Jesus as he said, "We know that you are a teacher who has come from God; for no one can do these signs that you do apart from the presence of God" (John 3:2).

Jesus knew that something more than a mere interest in him and his ministry was going on in Nicodemus's life. He picked up on that stirring within Nicodemus and confronted him immediately with a radical statement that seemed unrelated to what Nicodemus had talked about: "I tell you, no one can see the kingdom of God without being born from above" (John 3:3).

You can imagine that got Nicodemus's attention, so he asked, "How can anyone be born after having grown old? Can one enter a second time into the mother's womb and be born?" Jesus answered, "Very truly, I tell you, no one can enter the kingdom of God without being born of water and Spirit" (John 3:4-5).

Notice the inner-play on the words *wind* and *Spirit* as Jesus continued to explain what he was talking about:

> What is born of the flesh is flesh, and what is born of the Spirit is spirit. Do not be astonished that I said to you, "You must be born from above [or anew]." The wind [the same Greek word means both wind and Spirit] blows where it chooses, and you hear the sound of it, but you do not know where it comes from or where it goes. So it is with everyone who is born of the Spirit. (John 3:6-8)

In this story, what is reflected throughout Scripture comes through clearly. The Spirit brings life. Scripture says God breathed into Adam the breath of life; and as a result of that, Adam became a living being (Genesis 2:7). Again, we see the wordplay on wind (breath) and Spirit. The basic difference between a living and a dead human being is that the living one breathes and the dead one does not. So, at the heart of the Christian story is the fact that God breathes creation into being and breathes life into humankind. And in the Christian story, it follows that just as God brought Adam into life by breathing into him, so God is able to bring us to life and to bring the community of faith (the Church) to life through his Spirit today.

The Holy Spirit Brings Power

The Old Testament writers were people like us, always seeking ways to communicate truth and to testify to their experience. Like us, they were used to seeing things moved by an invisible force, the wind. They had seen trees bend under the force of the wind, and sand dunes built in the desert by the wind sweeping the earth from one place to another. And so they talked about the Spirit of God being like the wind, an unseen force that acted upon things and people. The Spirit of God was described as a surprising and even sometimes excessive power. As Theodore W. Jennings, Jr., has indicated, this wind of the Spirit sometimes *overwhelms* and at other times it *empowers* (p. 169).

Jennings also makes the point that the New Testament clarifies the meaning of the Spirit in the sense that it distinguishes between the spirit that overpowers (evil spirit) and the Spirit who empowers (Holy Spirit). That's a significant distinction.

The Holy Spirit empowers us to prevail over "alien spirits."

There are "spiritual forces" that overpower us in a destructive way. The New Testament refers to these spiritual forces as demons, and there is no hesitation in Scripture to deal with Satan, whom Paul called the Prince of Darkness. In his Letter to the Ephesians, Paul urged them to put on the whole armor of God to prepare themselves for battle: "For our struggle is not against enemies of blood and flesh, but against the rulers, against the authorities, against the cosmic powers of this present darkness, against the spiritual forces of evil in the heavenly places" (Ephesians 6:12).

The whole issue of evil and spiritual forces is an ongoing debate. But as we come to the close of the twentieth century, which was supposed to have been the century when "the age of enlightenment" would come to full flowering and human reason would push back the darkness and we would live in the light of a full-blossomed civilization, people are realizing that there are evil forces at work in the world and that human reason exercised fully is limited in what it has to offer.

This century has been the most devastating in the history of humankind—more people killed through wars and through inhumanity to one another than ever before. The great powers that we were going to use to make a perfect world have been used in such a way as to almost destroy the world.

And so, today, rational men and women of science are among those who are suggesting that maybe spiritual forces exist after all. We may be able to hold these spiritual forces in check if we remain vigilant and if we are aware of their powers, but we will not be able to eliminate them. We may talk about them however we wish and take the option of naming them however we will, but we shouldn't fail to recognize and acknowledge the fact that there is something in us, and outside us, something present in the world that is against us—a power that if we give in to it will slowly and systematically ruin our lives.

I have seen the Holy Spirit overpower those "alien spirits" by empowering persons with the very power of the living Christ. There was a young woman in a church I served for many years who was sexually abused by her father. She broke from that cycle of violence in her teens. For years she has lived with guilt and shame and depression, unable to free herself from destructive memories of that cruel violation. I knew only a little of her story. She was under psychiatric care and was receiving pastoral counseling from one of the ministers of the church. I observed that she always kept her distance from me. I didn't connect anything until on one occasion at a social reception I walked up to her from the side, put my hand on her shoulder, and greeted her. She reacted in a very emotional way, moving away from me as quickly as she could without a word.

Later, the minister who was counseling with her requested that he and the young woman come to see me together. I've never had such an experience. The woman's fear of me was very obvious. She almost tried to hide in the sofa, cowering back, holding the hand of the other minister. Gradually, in love the minister coaxed her into telling her story. Somehow, because of a slight physical likeness to her father, my presence triggered memories of her father and his violent violation of her life. She confessed that she had dreams of her father's abuse, and in those dreams, in a weird way she couldn't explain, she would see my face. She had shared that only with her psychiatrist and pastoral counselor, and they had been working with her for months. It was amazing that even in the security of that room, with her pastoral counselor seated beside her, she had great difficulty sharing in such close proximity with me.

I never will forget an experience about a month later. The church had an evening worship service that focused on praise, Holy Communion, and healing prayer. After receiving the sacrament, persons were invited to come as they wished to the altar for specific prayers with one of the ministers. Usually, people came to the minister nearest them. On this night, the young woman was not seated near me, but at the time when we called people to prayer, she almost ran across the front of the church and knelt before me. It was obvious that a power not her own was propelling her. She reached out to take my hands. Before that time, she would not have gotten within five feet of me. She began to pray. She expressed in prayer her experience of working through the alien spirits of shame and guilt and depression, feelings of worthlessness and uncleanness that had come from her being violated. The Holy Spirit prevailed over the alien power that had been controlling her life. This is a dramatic illustration of the Holy Spirit empowering us with the presence of Christ to prevail over alien spirits.

That experience reminded me of Jesus' healing of a man who was controlled by an "unclean spirit" (Luke 8:26-39):

> (For many times [the spirit] had seized him; he was kept under guard and bound with chains and shackles, but he would break the bonds and be driven by the demon into the wilds.) Jesus then asked him, "What is your name?" He said, "Legion"; for many demons had entered him. (Luke 8:29-30)

Jesus' power prevailed over spirits. The man was freed. When people came out to see what had happened, "they found the man from whom the demons had gone sitting at the feet of Jesus, clothed and in his right mind" (v. 35).

The same Christ, working in that man, was the Spirit working in the life of my friend.

The Holy Spirit empowers us to repent.

Consider the empowering dimension of the Holy Spirit's work in another way. It is connected with our becoming explicitly Christian, especially in what might be called adult conversion (that is, turning toward God and away from sin).

In the previous chapter we talked about what we do to receive the gracious love and forgiveness of God. We must see ourselves as we are and realize our need. A big part of that is the realization that we have sinned and that our sin is separating us from God, from our best selves, and from others. In that awareness, we repent; that is, we become deeply sorry for our sins.

It's easy to say that, to write those words, but it's a mammoth task to convince ourselves or to try to convince others that we are sinners. So the Holy Spirit works in our lives to convict us of our sin.

When Jesus was preparing his followers for his death, as indicated earlier, he promised them the Holy Spirit, an advocate of himself to be with them forever. And he made it clear that one of the things the Spirit would do would be to convict the world of its guilt and sin, and convince the world of the reality of judgment (John 16:7-11). Earlier in this chapter we acknowledged that the Holy Spirit came in a corporate way on a small company of first-century Christians. That story is told in the second chapter of Acts. After that dynamic invasion of the Holy Spirit, Peter preached to the crowds who were questioning the meaning of what was going on. He retold the story of God coming in Jesus Christ, how Jesus was crucified, and the fact that God had raised him from the dead. He concluded that message with a great proclamation: "God has made him both Lord and Messiah, this Jesus whom you crucified" (Acts 2:36).

When the crowd heard this, they were cut to the heart and asked, "What should we do?" Peter responded "Repent, and be baptized every one of you in the name of Jesus Christ so that your sins may be forgiven; and you will receive the gift of the Holy Spirit" (Acts 2:37-38).

Here is the word *repent.* It's one of those old-fashioned religious words that may have become distasteful to the modern mind because of the experiences persons have had with the call to repentance on the part of firebrand preachers. But that doesn't discredit the word. Today both psychology and medicine recognize the destructive forces involved in human emotions. Uncontrolled passions and emotions result in sinful behavior not because the passions and emotions are bad themselves but because they are invariably self-centered and uncontrolled. The Holy Spirit knew the depths of human evil long before Freud and the birth of depth psychology. And contemporary psychiatrists and psychologists are confessing that Freud, in maintaining that religion was an illusion, denied his patients the powerful therapy and curative force of confession and repentance.

Most of us have experienced it at some level—a confronting yet healing power not our own that causes us to become shamefully and painfully aware of our sin, of the destructive directions the undisciplined life is taking. And we have also experienced a power not our own that enables us to become humble and free from our pride and arrogance to the point that we will willingly share with another and eventually confess to God and express our desire to go in another direction.

That's the work of the Holy Spirit—overpowering our pride, self-assurance, arrogance, and self-centeredness by empowering us to repentance—empowering us to become humble and repentant.

The Holy Spirit empowers us to cope.

I have seen it many times—persons who are transformed from people who are helpless objects of forces beyond their control into dynamic, active, decision-making persons who participate in the ministry and mission of Christ. They are in control of their lives because by their testimony they are controlled by the Spirit.

I have a friend who is spending two years in prison. She was converted about two years before she was arrested, being implicated in drug dealing by relation and association with her father, who was a drug lord and has been imprisoned for life. Jane (not her real name) insists, and I believe, that she is innocent. We have corresponded during the time of her imprisonment, and I have seen a powerful transformation. As I write this, she has four more months to serve; then she will be in a halfway house for six months. In her last letter, she wrote:

> The things I have learned throughout this experience I will never forget. As painful as it has been, I now see it as an important, perhaps necessary step in my breakthrough to a happier life.
>
> For one thing I have been profoundly humbled. I see that "of myself I am nothing." So when I had finally had enough and couldn't take it anymore I realized there had to be a better way—that's where *God* came in. The moment of surrender is not when life is over. It's when it begins. . . .
>
> All of a sudden I am not too proud to ask for help, *God's* help and guidance.
>
> I feel fortunate and very grateful to have gotten a second chance at life. I am so excited! This is the absolute best *HIGH* I have ever known. Totally awesome!!!
>
> Thinking of you and looking at life through new eyes. . . .

How do you explain that but by the empowerment of the Holy Spirit?

The Holy Spirit empowers us to forgive.

In her book *The Hiding Place,* Corrie ten Boom tells about the forgiving power of the Holy Spirit operating in her life. After her release from a concentration camp where her sister died, she lectured and preached all over the world about the need to forgive our enemies. She was confronted by her own message in a stunning experience. Following one of her sermons, she was greeted by a man whom she recognized as the S.S. guard at the "shower room" at the concentration camp. Suddenly, it was all there—the roomful of mocking men, the heaps of clothing, her sister Betsie's pain-blanched face.

> He came up to me as the church was emptying, beaming and bowing. "How grateful I am for your message, Fraulein," he said. "To think that, as you say, He has washed my sins away!"

His hand was thrust out to shake mine. And I, who had preached so often to the people in Bloemendaal the need to forgive, kept my hand at my side.

Even as the angry, vengeful thoughts boiled through me, I saw the sin of them. Jesus Christ had died for this man; was I going to ask for more? Lord Jesus, I prayed, forgive me and help me to forgive him.

I tried to smile. I struggled to raise my hand. I could not. I felt nothing, not the slightest spark of warmth or charity. And so again I breathed a silent prayer. Jesus, I cannot forgive him. Give me Your forgiveness.

As I took his hand a most incredible thing happened. From my shoulder along my arm and through my hand a current seemed to pass from me to him, while into my heart sprang a love for this stranger that almost overwhelmed me.

And so I discovered that it is not on our forgiveness any more than on our goodness that the world's healing hinges, but on His. When He tells us to love our enemies, He gives, along with the command, the love itself. (ten Boom, p. 215)

It's not easy to forgive; we know that. Corrie ten Boom confessed empowerment beyond herself was at work. Love was given by the Christ who told her to love her enemies, and the Holy Spirit empowered her to put that love into practice by forgiving.

The Holy Spirit empowers us to bear all the burdens of life.

I Know Why the Caged Bird Sings is Maya Angelou's beautiful and moving autobiography. James Baldwin said of it, "Her portrait is a biblical study of life in the midst of death." Her grandmother was a powerful person in her life. Early in the book she shares one incident that gives a clear picture of the burden of life. Her people had been oppressed and pushed down into the backwaters of life. She told of the time when a troop of "the powhitetrash kids" came to her grandmother's store and mocked her grandmother in all sorts of ways, aping the way she stood, trying to mimic her facial expressions, crossing their eyes and sticking their thumbs in both sides of their mouths to stretch them into awful expressions of mockery. One of the girls, the oldest and the tallest, even did a handstand before the elderly black woman, and when her dress fell around her face with her heels up, she had no underpants—the most indecent mockery that could have been inflicted on that woman. The other girls clapped as this one finished her handstand.

All the time, the elderly woman had been singing. Now she changed her song to "Bread of Heaven, bread of Heaven, feed me till I want no more." Maya Angelou tells the story from that point in this fashion:

> I found that I was praying too. How long could Momma hold out? What new indignity would they think of to subject her to? Would I be able to stay out of it? What would Momma really like me to do?
>
> Then they were moving out of the yard, on their way to town. They bobbed their heads and shook their slack behinds and turned, one at a time:
>
> "'Bye, Annie."
>
> "'Bye, Annie."
>
> "'Bye, Annie."
>
> Momma never turned her head or unfolded her arms, but she stopped singing and said, "'Bye, Miz Helen, 'bye, Miz Ruth, 'bye, Miz Eloise."
>
> I burst. . . . Why couldn't she have come inside the sweet, cool store when we saw them breasting the hill? What did she prove? And then if they were dirty, mean and impudent, why did Momma have to call them Miz?
>
> She stood singing another whole song through and then opened the screen door to look down on me crying in rage. She looked until I looked up. Her face was a brown moon that shone on me. She was beautiful. Something had happened out there, which I couldn't completely understand, but I could see that she was happy. Then she bent down and touched me as mothers of the church "lay hands on the sick and afflicted" and I quieted.
>
> "Go wash your face, Sister." And she went behind the candy counter and hummed, "Glory, glory, hallelujah, when I lay my burden down."
>
> . . . Whatever the contest had been out front, I knew Momma had won. (Angelou, pp. 26-27)

The Holy Spirit gives us the power to bear the burdens of life. In his preparation to leave the disciples, Jesus promised to send them the Holy Spirit. The Greek word for "Holy Spirit" is translated variously "Comforter," "Advocate," or "Counselor," all indicating the empowering presence of the Holy Spirit.

Summary

We experience God as Father, Son, and Holy Spirit. As Jesus, God's Son, reveals what God is like, the Holy Spirit empowers us to live as Jesus calls us to live. We must not forget that the Spirit is the Spirit of the Father and the Son.

The New Testament Christian community, and Christians since then, experience the presence of the Spirit as the pledge of our total salvation and the ultimate triumph of God over all principalities and powers, over all creation. Paul put it this way: God "put his Spirit in our hearts as a deposit, guaranteeing what is to come" (2 Corinthians 1:22 NIV; see also 2 Corinthians 5:5; Ephesians 1:14).

The Greek word for "deposit" is often translated as "pledge" or "surety." It is an unusual word, and language authorities say that it was probably derived from Phoenician traders. Its basic meaning is "down payment" or "token of commitment." We can understand that kind of language because in our commercial dealings, we often make a down payment to secure possession of something. The deposit promises that there is more payment to come, but it also ensures that we become the possessors, the owners of it *now*.

It is a rather descriptive designation of the activity of the Spirit in our lives. God's gift of the Spirit demonstrates, like a wedding band, that we belong to him, but it is also a pledge that there is more to come. All that has come before in the history of salvation—from creation, covenant, law, and prophets to the wonders of the incarnation in Christ—is here recapitulated, both as promise and as possession. The Spirit gives us concrete and sometimes dramatic signs that God's promise to renew all of creation is going to take place. The Spirit provides us signs and indications that our faith is not in vain, that promises of God are not fantasies, and that our hope is really based on reality.

The Holy Spirit is intimately connected with the Church and the presence of the Church in the world, as well as the gifts that are ours to live the Christian life, and the signs of our maturing as Christians that are sometimes called "fruit of the Spirit." We will look at both dynamics of the Spirit in the next two chapters.

CHAPTER FIVE

THE CHURCH

What is the Church?

Lewis Grizzard was a syndicated newspaper columnist, the author of a number of books, and a rather sophisticated writer who pretended to be a redneck. He was brash, irreverent, and sometimes obscene. I often felt that he was laughing at something, such as his failure in three marriages, to keep from crying. He came off in most of his columns as crusty and tough, but now and then he wrote of some of the heart issues of life and communicated a profound depth of understanding and a winsome tenderness.

In one of his columns, Grizzard wrote about the Church. He described standing outside the church in his hometown of Moreland, Georgia, on a cold day. It had been at least ten years since he had been inside, but there were still roots there.

As he reminisced about the youth group that met on Sunday nights, he recounted how two rowdy boys in town broke into a store and were required to attend the youth group for six months as punishment. The first night they attended, Grizzard recalled, they beat up two boys and threw a hymnal at the nice woman who led the group and always brought cookies. Fortunately, she ducked just in time. Grizzard remembered her words to the boys: "I don't approve of what you boys did here tonight, and neither does Jesus. But if He can forgive you, I guess I can too." Then she handed them the plate of cookies. The last Grizzard heard, both boys had grown up to become "good daddies with steady jobs" who rarely miss a Sunday in church. He concluded that it was the first miracle he ever saw.

Whatever our experience, there is no Christianity apart from the Church. This is true because there is no such thing as solitary Christianity. Although our Christian faith and experience must be personal, they cannot be private. The more private we seek to make them, the more distorted they become. Jesus' life and ministry were never matters of private religious feelings that he kept to himself: He lived his life for others. A personal experience of Christ kept private soon dies.

Jesus promised his presence in community: "Where two or three are gathered in my name, I am there among them" (Matthew 18:20). The birth of the Church was the first act of the Holy Spirit after the resurrection and ascension of Jesus. The crucifixion of Jesus had shattered the dreams of his followers. They were confused and frustrated, not knowing what was going on and what the future held. They were filled with fear; and within only a few days after Jesus' death, some of his original twelve disciples returned to their former way of life.

Jesus appeared to them after his resurrection, and he ordered them not to leave Jerusalem but to wait there for the promise of the Father. "This," he said, "is what you have heard from me; for John baptized with water, but you will be baptized with the Holy Spirit not many days from now" (Acts 1:4-5).

As detailed in the last chapter, the Holy Spirit came upon that little group gathered in an upper room in Jerusalem. The Spirit came because they *obeyed* Jesus, stayed together, and waited for the promise. Again, the Spirit and Christ cannot be separated. It was there that the Church was born. There would have been no Church, no Christian community, had there been no Resurrection and had the promised Holy Spirit not been given. So, *the Church is a gathering of people who have experienced Christ as the risen Lord.*

What is the Church all about?

A man in a congregation I once served, though married and the father of three children, was a homosexual. Tom (not his real name) had been arrested for aggressive overt behavior and was under the care of a psychiatrist. Only his wife knew. Then he confided in me. He was finding meaning in his marriage, and his homosexual tendencies were latent; yet he felt unworthy, guilt-ridden, impotent in interpersonal relations, verging on becoming a recluse. I invited him to share with me in a small men's prayer-share group that met weekly—promising, of course, to keep his confidence. People began to care about him, to share their lives with him, and he began to blossom as a person.

Finally, Tom got the courage to share privately with another man in the group. I was surprised when he told me about it. The other man was a picture of masculinity, almost an exaggerated masculinity (chauvinistic, some might say)—the last person I would have thought would understand Tom's struggle. But he did understand. He accepted Tom and continued to love him; and redemption took place. Tom emerged from guilt and self-condemnation and became a dynamic, redemptive force in that church. He was loved and accepted into being by the grace of Christ working through another man and a small group. That small group of men was the Church.

The Body of Christ

When we hear the word *church*, we may think of a building at the corner of Elm and Main or the congregation to which we belong or our particular denomination. We may think of a building, an institution, or the newest assembly of Christians in our community. The early Christians knew themselves to be an assembly of people given birth by the Holy Spirit *to be the presence of Christ in the world.* That was their purpose: to be and do all that Christ was and did when he was among us in the flesh. As Jesus was the incarnation of God, God's fully human presence in the world, so the Church is a continuation of the Incarnation—as the presence of Christ in the world today, empowered by the Spirit.

A dominant image of the Church in the New Testament is the Body of Christ. Paul is the champion of this image. When Jesus was raised from the dead, Paul said:

> [God] seated him at his right hand in the heavenly places, far above all rule and authority and power and dominion, and above every name that is named, not only in this age but also in the age to come. And he has put all things under his feet and has made him the head over all things for the church, which is his body, the fullness of him who fills all in all. (Ephesians 1:20-23)

In this particular passage, Paul tries to communicate the breadth of Christ's power. It is *resurrection power*—the power of God "accomplished in Christ when he raised him from the dead" (v. 20 RSV). It is *ascension* power—"seated him at his right hand in the heavenly places" (v. 20). It is *dominion* power—"far above all rule and authority and power and dominion. . . . And he has put all things under his feet and has made him the head over all things for the church" (vv. 21-22). In these three phrases Paul pours out his surging soul as he seeks to do the impossible—to capture in words the immeasurable power and glory of God's work in Christ.

Paul's Letter to the Ephesians has been called the Epistle of the Ascension. It is that because here we meet the exalted power of Christ. The early Christians were post-Resurrection, post-Ascension Christians. They knew the gospel story: Jesus was once a baby in his mother's arms—but not now; Jesus was a carpenter, teacher, companion, and friend—but not now; his healing love mercifully blessed all he touched, all he could see and hear and speak to—but he is not limited by time and space now; as a self-giving Suffering Servant he hung on a cross, pouring out his life and love on our behalf—but he is not hanging there now. God raised him from the dead!

The character of Jesus' person and work has not changed; but now it is spread abroad through the Church in the power of the Spirit in a way that it never would have been if everything had continued to depend on Jesus' presence. Jesus ascended, and the curtain went up on a new act in the drama. Pentecost happened. The Spirit of this ascended One was poured out on his followers, and the Church was born. Paul writes that the ascended One is "far above all rule and authority and power and dominion." His name is exalted "above every name that is named, not only in this age but also in the age to come." Everything has been put under Jesus' feet. He is the head, the authority. He has been given dominion. And the Church is his Body—"the fullness of him who fills all in all."

What an exciting notion to seek to fulfill: The Church is the Body of Christ! The very Spirit that dwelt in Jesus dwells in the Church. The very power that raised Jesus from the tomb is available to God's people.

As God's people, the Church, given birth by the Holy Spirit after Jesus' crucifixion and resurrection, more than anything else is a community of incarnation and resurrection. It is composed of people who know the forces of sin and sin's deadly power in their lives but who have experienced the forgiveness, the justification, the reconciliation, and the liberation of the risen Christ. The Church as the Body of Christ, as Christ's presence in the world, seeks to be and do all that Christ was and did when he was among us as a physical presence.

The Covenant Community

Because the Church is the Body of Christ, it is God's idea rather than a human idea. God's revelation continues. God chose Israel to be God's people, to be a "light to the nations." In the New Testament, the Christian community is referred to as the new Israel. In his first epistle, Peter writes,

> But you are a chosen race, a royal priesthood, a holy nation, God's own people, that you may declare the wonderful deeds of him who called you out of darkness into his marvelous light. Once you were no people but now you are God's people; once you had not received mercy but now you have received mercy.
> (1 Peter 2:9-10 RSV)

Peter was writing to Christians who were in dispersion, facing slander and persecution. It was a circular letter to be passed from group to group. Its purpose was to fortify the Christians and enable them to stand fast in their Christian commitment. So, Peter sought to give them strength and courage by reminding them of who they were.

This passage of Peter is rooted in the Old Testament concept of the covenant. The people of God were those people with whom God had made a covenant. The tenth verse can be seen as a fulfillment of the prophet Hosea recording God's promise: "I will have mercy upon her that had not obtained mercy; and I will say to them which were not my people, Thou art my people; and they shall say, Thou art my God" (Hosea 2:23 KJV). Peter remembered that word and quoted it almost verbatim.

Peter applied title after title to this "no people" who had been called into life by the grace of God. He designated them "a chosen race, a royal priesthood, a holy nation." All these phrases are the great designations of the people of Israel in the Old Testament. The promise that God made to Israel, the covenant of relationship, is fulfilled in the Church. This is the new Israel, the new covenant community.

So the Church is God's idea. The phrase translated "God's people" literally means "a people of God's possession." The King James Version translates it "a peculiar people." As Christians, our relationship to God is unique. We are God's people, God's possession. God said to Israel, "This people have I formed for myself; they shall show forth my praise" (Isaiah 43:21 KJV).

A Home of Grace

As the Church, then, we are the people of God or the household of faith. These images suggest home and family—people belonging to one another because we belong to Christ. In that fellowship, we find acceptance, forgiveness, healing, and relationship. The fellowship becomes a redemptive power within the lives of those who are a part of it and extends that redemption beyond itself.

Using the image of the Christian congregation as a family of faith, the *home* becomes a dynamic symbol. If grace is one of the defining characteristics of God, if Jesus' ministry reflected the gracious activity of God in human life, then the Church is a home of grace. The poet Robert Frost wrote, "Home is the place where, when you have to go there, they have to take you in." Home is "something you somehow haven't to deserve." That's a good picture of the Church.

The Church is a home of grace. It is the only institution I know where the requirement for joining is that you are not worthy to be a member.

The point of the Bible is not that we are perfect or that we should be perfect in the way we normally define that word. The point of the Bible is that God is gracious. The more I try to be perfect, the more my behavior proves otherwise. Have you experienced it as I have? The more I try to prove that I am "good" and sinless, the more guilty I feel; and the more guilty I feel, the harder I work at proving I am not. So the whole matter becomes a vicious circle in which I can't win. It feeds upon itself like some sickness.

All we can do is what Isaiah and Peter did. In the Temple, the prophet Isaiah cried out, "Woe is me! I am lost, for I am a man of unclean lips, and I live among a people of unclean lips" (Isaiah 6:5). And when Jesus instructed Peter to cast his nets on the other side of the boat, he caught so many fish that his nets were breaking and his boat was sinking. It was then that Peter knew what was going on. He fell on his knees at Jesus' feet and said, "Go away from me, Lord, for I am a sinful man!" (Luke 5:8).

All we can do is confess who we are, that we are not perfect, that we are sinners, and trust God's grace. When we do that, we finally discover that God is not interested in punishing us. God is waiting and wanting to empower us, to enable us to live the kind of life God has created for us.

In the worship services of a church I served, we often had a lay witness. One fellow shared the following testimony:

I used to think that miracles only happened in the Bible, but I know now that miracles are happening all around us every day. Having been raised in a Christian home, I was accustomed to Jesus being a part of my everyday life, but as I grew older I gradually drifted away from God.

My first marriage ended in divorce. My wife took our daughter away . . . and married my best friend. After eleven years, my second marriage was over too. I had long since lost her to alcohol before she ended her life in a sea of loneliness and despair; and I held absolutely no hope for my future. I was forty-one years old and my life was a mess.

I started coming to Singles Fellowship here . . . where my life was changed forever. In this setting, God, through these people, reached out and met me where I was. They were the true Body of Christ, wrapping me in his loving arms. I was unconditionally accepted just as I was, and I was not judged by my past. A special unexplainable warmth began to grow inside of me, and I was brought to a new beginning.

I became more and more active and the more involved I became, the more blessings I received. My cup filled up real fast and then started to spill out. I found that the more I shared with a humble heart, the more my cup overflowed . . .

I am not proud of a lot of things I did in my past, but God is using that "experience" as a special ministry to others. Time is so precious and there's so much to be done. This church is alive as the Body of Christ and I am grateful that the reason is because this church is not a fortress for saints. For me, it is a place where a broken life was mended, where a shattered dream gave way to a new hope, and where true healing took place. It's also a place where I can come and openly affirm the God who cares for each and every one of us. Finally, it's a place where I can *shout* and *sing* and *thank* the God who shared his grace with me. Even though I don't deserve it, I have it anyway!

God is good!
All the time!

This man has experienced the Church as a home of grace.

Dame Edith Sitwell said of William Blake, the great painter and poet, "Of course he was cracked. That's where the light shone through." I like that explanation! All of us are cracked somewhere, or we are not what we are cracked up to be. None of us are perfect and will never be. It is the knowledge of our imperfection, the willingness to know that we are flawed, that becomes our asset. When we recognize that, we are in the position to receive the power to be what we are called to be as individuals and as the Church.

A favorite hymn of many people is "Amazing Grace." The story of its author, John Newton, is a thrilling one. Newton was the captain of a slave ship. Ironically, the slave ship was called *The Jesus.* The flourishing slave trade was a great shame of Western civilization for over a hundred years. For Newton, however, it was just a job. It was all he had ever known. Following in his father's footsteps, he went to sea when he was eleven years old.

As an adult, something began to stir inside him. The inhumanity inflicted on human beings by the slave industry began to burn in his consciousness, and he knew it wasn't right. It offended him and created a raging restlessness in his conscience.

Then it happened. One day, Newton was in Liverpool, England, and he went to a little Methodist church and was converted. The evidence of his conversion was that he became an abolitionist in a time and a country in which abolition was an unpopular cause. He joined others in the battle against slavery, what John Wesley called the "vilest sin under the sun." Newton wrote the hymn "Amazing Grace" to tell the story of his transformation and to express the centrality of the Christian's faith.

It is no wonder that this is a favorite hymn. It gathers up one of the most profound facets of the gospel—the saving grace of Jesus Christ.

> Amazing grace! How sweet the sound
> that saved a wretch like me!
> I once was lost, but now am found;
> was blind, but now I see.

That gospel of grace defines and shapes the Church as a home of grace.

A Home for All

Newsweek magazine carried the story of the memorial service held for Hubert Humphrey, former vice president of the United States. Hundreds of people came from all over the world to say good-bye to their old friend and colleague. But one person who came was shunned and ignored by virtually everyone there. Nobody would look at him, much less speak to him. That person was former president Richard Nixon. Not long before, he had gone through the shame and infamy of Watergate. He was back in Washington for the first time since his resignation from the presidency.

Then a very special thing happened, perhaps the only thing that could have made a difference and broken the ice. President Jimmy Carter, who was in the White House at that time, came into the room. Before he was seated, he saw Nixon over against the wall, all by himself. He went over to Nixon as though he were greeting a family member, stuck out his hand to the former president, and smiled broadly. To the surprise of everybody there, the two of them embraced each other, and Carter said, "Welcome home, Mr. President! Welcome back home again!"

Commenting on the scene, *Newsweek* magazine asserted, "If there was a turning point in Nixon's long ordeal in the wilderness, it was that moment and that gesture of love and compassion."

That simple, but profound, gesture of acceptance and hospitality speaks volumes. If the Christian gospel is not for everyone, it is not worthy of anyone. If the Church is not a home for all, it is not a home at all.

A Home for New Life

As a home of grace and a home for all, the Church is a home for new life.

I received a letter from a young man, a university graduate student, who has new life in Christ because he found the Church to be a home of grace and a home for all. He talked about a special relationship that had brought almost unbearable pain and left him emotionally disabled. He described it as the kind of relationship "that numbs someone, leads them to fear new relationships, and allows this devil we oh-so-often deny to keep us still when our Lord would have us in motion."

He then talked about his experience in the worship of the congregation and the new relationships enriching his life:

On the flip side, it is the voice of peers, who cannot possibly understand the devilish complexities that have torn apart past relationships, that asks "why are you still single?" and says "you should have no problem finding someone."

Well, I found someone all right. His name is Jesus, and he does understand my longing to give of myself to others, though it is not money I'm able to give. He understands a rural-town boy who endures little indignities in a big city university for his desire to learn what they have to teach, yet apply it to a music that praises God and fills the soul. He understands someone who has been in a string of relationships with "significant others" who could not comprehend why I would do my utmost to love them just as they are—and left because I was too close, gave too much, and stubbornly refused to understand why they would shut me out and leave. He understands someone who doesn't "circulate" very well in a crowded room, someone who sings a simple song for Jesus, someone who remains silent when most others are speaking . . . Jesus understands.

In the New Testament, the apostle Paul writes about the power of the Resurrection in our personal lives and in the Church. In Colossians 2:6, he writes, "As you therefore have received Christ Jesus the Lord, continue to live your lives in him." He follows this by reminding us that we were buried with Christ in baptism and also were raised with him through faith (Colossians 2:12). It is tragic that many Christian congregations do not see themselves as a community of resurrection, of new life. As much as anything, local congregations need to know who they are.

A congregation I served worked for over a year grappling with its identity and writing a mission statement. We experienced it as an exciting and challenging statement for the purpose of the church. The mission statement began by affirming the church's identity, which determines the church's function.

As the Body of Christ, we are called to
- *Celebrate* Christ in worship,
- *Honor* Christ in all we do,
- *Reveal* Christ in our witness and fellowship,
- *Instruct* persons for discipleship and ministry,
- *Serve* persons in Christ's name, and
- *Transform* the world by spreading scriptural holiness.

The church's identity is the Body of Christ. The church is the presence of Christ in the world—a community of resurrection, new life. That calls members to worship—to celebrate Christ in worship. Who or what we worship defines who or what we are.

Why should a Christian attend worship?

In one of his novels, William Faulkner wrote, "That which is destroying the Church is not the outward groping of those within it or the inward groping of those without, but the professionals who control it and have removed the bells from its steeples."

I don't know everything Faulkner meant by that, but this seems clear: Steeple bells were meant to call people to worship. Worship is at the heart of what the church is about.

Worship Is Remembering

Worship is rehearsing the mighty acts of God. The poet said, "God gives us memory that we may have roses in December." Memory plays a powerful role in our lives. It's a source of healing. We can be healed from depression if we can retain our capacity to remember. We can get through some of the tough conflicts in our marriages if we will only remember how it was when we first loved each other, when we committed ourselves to each other, and when we had not yet become dull and prosaic and calloused to the mystery and meaning of being made one in spirit and in flesh.

So, worshiping is remembering—it is summoning the past into the present. It is rehearsing the mighty acts of God.

We live in constant forgetfulness of God. Halford Luccock, a pastor, author, and columnist, wrote about a young man who lived and worked in a pretty tough environment. He tried to hold on to his religion when people were cruel to him. He was not always appreciated for his religious views, and people made fun of him. They were always challenging him and his commitment. One day a particularly abusive person said, "You damn fool, can't you see if there is a God who cares a penny for the likes of you, God would tell someone to come along and give you what you need—decent food, a bed for yourself, at least a chance to make good."

The young man replied, "I reckon God does tell someone, but someone always forgets."

We live in constant forgetfulness of God. So, when we come to worship, we remember.

One of the most beautiful words of Jesus, and one of the most redemptive words Paul recalled, is in 1 Corinthians 11:24. Jesus was spending his last days with his disciples. They were celebrating the Passover, that signal event in the Jewish faith when the community recalls God's mighty act of delivering the people out of Egyptian bondage. Jesus baptized that Passover with even more poignant meaning, saying to them, "Do this in remembrance of me." And he said that to them after he had told them that he was going to the cross. In worship, we remember and rehearse the mighty acts of God. We summon the past into the present and are empowered.

Worship Is Transformation

A woman said to her pastor, "Pastor, I just don't know what to do. I grew up Methodist but became dissatisfied;

became a Baptist but that grew old; I've been a Presbyterian and an Episcopalian. . . . I just don't know what I am!"

The wise but blunt pastor replied, "Don't worry, my dear, it doesn't matter what label is on an empty bottle!"

Simply being religious is not the answer. Worshiping just to have good feelings and to find some comfort or some escape from the world is alien to what true worship is all about.

I think of the Branch Davidian tragedy near Waco, Texas, in 1993, which claimed the attention of our entire nation for weeks. The FBI went to war with a religious community. It was frustrating to see the loyalty and devotion of people to such a flawed understanding of Christianity. At the time of the confrontation, when cult members had barricaded themselves in their compound, a cartoon on the editorial page of a daily newspaper showed two groups: a congregation sleeping while a pastor preached, and a cult group on the edge of their seats, intently listening to their leader. The caption said, "The difference between church members and cult members." How disturbing and how sad! What is the difference? It has to do with commitment. To be sure, the Branch Davidians had a distorted notion, but who could question their commitment? Commitment to that degree, shaped and defined by Christian worship, brings transformation.

In worship, we remember God the Father, God the Son, and God the Holy Spirit are one. We rehearse God's mighty acts in history. We remember that the risen Christ is alive through the power of the Holy Spirit; and because Christ is in our worship in the power of the Holy Spirit, we are empowered and transformed.

I have witnessed this transformation many times, because Christ has been present in worship in the power of the Holy Spirit.

A husband forsook his wife after the children were grown, selfishly and sinfully abandoned her for some "young thing," broke her heart, crushed her spirit, and left her lifeless. But in the Church, by the power of the living Christ, she found life.

Men and women controlled by their addictions, lost in a wasteland of despair and endless repetition of loss and failure, found their higher power in Jesus Christ and were living free and with purpose.

Persons who sought meaning in their jobs and professions, in accumulating money and being secure, found themselves at the top, but there was no encore, nothing else different to do, nowhere else to go, and their lives still lacked meaning. Then, in the Church, they found a commitment to others, to poor and oppressed people, that challenged them. They helped build a home for God's working poor people, or they went on a mission trip; and meaning unlike anything they had known came to them. They discovered a life-style of serving that added a new dimension to their lives.

Summary

Forgiveness from sin, reconciliation of relationship, deliverance from all sorts of bondage, freedom from the dead end and meaningless selfishness and materialism—the Church is all of this and more. The Church is a congregation of Spirit-touched, Spirit-led, Spirit-empowered people who perpetuate the Incarnation. The Church, then, is not a place or a building. It is more an organism than an organization. It is not static but lively and dynamic. It is an assembly of people with a common purpose—persons in whom Christ dwells by the presence of the Holy Spirit, coming together in worship, ministry, and fellowship. It is "home"—home of grace, home for all, and home for new life.

CHAPTER SIX

BEING CHRISTIAN

What does it mean to be a Christian?

I don't know any person in our contemporary time who demonstrates the meaning of being a Christian as powerfully and as transparently as Mother Teresa. We see Christ in her. When I ask audiences around the nation to name the one person who best communicates the meaning of the Christian life, by far the most frequently mentioned person is Mother Teresa.

Mother Teresa came to Memphis a few years ago to dedicate a convent and a mission of her community of charity. There was a great worship service and celebration of Mass in the Coliseum. My wife and I were invited to share in the service. One of the most amazing things to me was what happened to over eight thousand people when Mother Teresa and the nuns entered the Coliseum. It was amazing because it contrasted so sharply with what usually happened in the Coliseum. I'm a basketball fan, and I went to all the basketball games I could there. I also attended concerts at the Coliseum, and each time it was bedlam—applause, screaming, yelling—the ultimate in noisy, enthusiastic response to what was going on. But when Mother Teresa and the sisters came out on the floor of the Coliseum, a holy hush descended on that crowd. You could hear the nuns walking on the floor; had they not been walking, you could have heard a pin drop. It was a kind of eerie hush that spoke of reverence and awe. The tiny, stoop-backed, wrinkled-faced woman evoked that holy hush from a mass of people.

I know people's response to Mother Teresa is to what they know about her ministry—but I can't help believing it's also to her very being, her person. She is humility incarnate. Throughout that two-hour Mass, she was obviously in prayer most of the time. For a good part of the time, she was completely removed from what was going on around her. Often, she became even more stooped as she rested her elbows on her knees and cradled her head in her hands, lost in deep prayer.

After the Mass, she spoke. She spoke simply, but her words penetrated the conscience of the audience because her words flowed out of a life of prayer and service. She called us to prayer and to a life of tender mercy, which she said are inseparable. She punctuated her brief talks with some personal experiences. She told of walking on the streets of Calcutta and seeing something moving in a ditch. She had to look carefully to see that it was an emaciated man—still alive, his whole body covered with worms. She took him back to their center that cares for dying persons. It took the sisters three hours to pick the worms off the man, then they bathed him, gave him some simple food, and introduced him to love— love and prayer with no strings attached.

The man died. But he died with dignity, knowing that he was loved, which is really the ministry of Mother Teresa and her sisters. As he lay dying, he looked up at Mother Teresa and said, "I came here as an animal. I leave in death as an angel." And he smiled and died.

When I had an opportunity to greet Mother Teresa after the service, her deep compassionate eyes and her simple word of blessing touched my soul. I understood, in that brief encounter, how she became the influence of conversion for Malcolm Muggeridge.

Muggeridge was a newspaperman in Great Britain and an antagonist of the Church. Late in life, primarily through the influence of Mother Teresa, he was converted to Christianity and became a powerful defender of the faith. He described Mother Teresa in this fashion:

> In the dismal slums of Calcutta . . . Mother Teresa and her Missionaries of Charity go about Jesus's work of love with incomparable dedication. When I think of them, as I have seen them at work and at their devotion, I want to put away all the books, tear up all the scribbled notes. There are no more doubts or dilemmas; everything is perfectly clear. What commentary or exposition, however eloquent, lucid, perceptive, inspired even, can equal in elucidation and illumination the effect of these dedicated lives? What mind has conceived a discourse, or tongue spoken it, which conveys even to a minute degree the light they shine before men? *I was an hungred, and ye gave me meat; I was thirsty, and ye gave me drink: I was a stranger, and ye took me: naked and ye clothed me: I was sick, and ye visited me: I was in prison, and ye came unto me*—the words come alive, as no study or meditation could possibly make them, in the fulfilment in the most literal sense of Jesus's behest to see in the suffering face of humanity his suffering face, and in their broken bodies, his. . . .
>
> In the face of a Mother Teresa I trace the very geography of Jesus's Kingdom; all the contours and valleys and waterways. I need no other map. (Muggeridge, pp. 71, 73)

It is no wonder that someone wrote of her, "First she gave her life to Christ, then through Christ to her neighbor. That was the end of her biography and the beginning of her life."

Mother Teresa shows us so clearly that being Christian is being Christ in the world, living as Christ in our daily relationships. Martin Luther was convinced that Christians are to be "little Christs." Again, it is a continuation of the Incarnation. The apostle Paul said, "God was in Christ reconciling the world to Himself." He talked about the Church being the

Body of Christ—a continuation of the incarnation of God in Jesus Christ. He also designated our ministry as a continuation of the Incarnation: "God was in Christ reconciling the world to himself, . . . and has given us the ministry of reconciliation" (2 Corinthians 5:19, 18 NKJV). *What Christ has been and done for us, as Christians we must be and do for the world.* What does it mean to communicate Christ's presence to others? It would be difficult to spell it out in detail in the scope of one chapter, but perhaps a general sketch will help to present a picture of what it means to be a "little Christ" to the world.

Discipleship

Two biblical images of people of faith are useful as we seek to understand what being Christian means. The two images are *disciple* and *pilgrim.* As disciples, we are apprenticed to our Master, Jesus Christ. A disciple is a learner, not in an academic sort of way, but in the same way that one is an apprentice to a craftsperson—learning the craft at the work site while doing the actual work. So, as Christians, we are always in a growing-learning relationship with Jesus Christ. The image of a pilgrim adds to the meaning of being a disciple because it suggests that we are going someplace; we are on a journey. We are journeying to God, and on that journey we walk in the company of Jesus, who is our guide.

When Jesus wanted to define the meaning of discipleship, he expressed it emphatically: "If any want to become my followers, let them deny themselves and take up their cross and follow me" (Matthew 16:24). A story in the New Testament clarifies this call of Jesus. A young rich man, a ruler of the people, came to Jesus and asked, "What shall I do to inherit eternal life?" Jesus told him to keep the commandments. He responded that he had kept the commandments— that was the desire of his life, and he was committed to doing that. But Jesus, always perceptive about persons, made this piercing observation: "You still lack one thing. Sell all that you have and distribute to the poor, and you will have treasure in heaven." And he added this invitation: "Come, follow Me" (Luke 18:18-22 NKJV).

On another occasion, Jesus put the demands of discipleship in this fashion: "He who loves his life will lose it, and he who hates his life in this world will keep it for eternal life. If anyone serves Me, let him follow Me" (John 12:25-26 NKJV).

So the call is clear—it is a call to walk with Jesus, to be a pilgrim, to be his disciple. This requires our obedience.

Obedience

I've come to believe that the primary way that we become Christian, "little Christs" in the world, is by our obedience to the Holy Spirit. The Holy Spirit enables us to live our way into Christlikeness. I have never seen persons who studied or thought their way into Christlikeness, nor have I known persons who prayed or worshiped their way into Christlikeness. Yet, I've seen countless persons who acted and lived their way into Christlikeness. The likeness of Christ shines forth from their lives. Now to be sure, they pray; many of them are people with a deep prayer life. They study to varying degrees, and they worship. But most of all, they are people who seek diligently to live the way Christ lived, and their actions have caused them to grow to look like Jesus.

One of the most beautiful descriptions of Jesus in Scripture is found in Philippians 2:

> Let the same mind be in you that was in Christ Jesus,
> who, though he was in the form of God,
> did not regard equality with God
> as something to be exploited,
> but emptied himself,
> taking the form of a slave,
> being born in human likeness.

And being found in human form,
   he humbled himself
   and became obedient to the point of death—
   even death on a cross.

Therefore God also highly exalted him
   and gave him the name
   that is above every name,
so that at the name of Jesus
   every knee should bend,
   in heaven and on earth and under the earth,
and every tongue should confess
   that Jesus Christ is Lord,
   to the glory of God the Father. (Philippians 2:5-11)

While this is a beautiful and vivid description of who Jesus is, it also is a call to us: "Let this mind be in you, which was also in Christ Jesus: who . . . took upon him the form of a servant . . . and became obedient unto death, even the death of the cross" (KJV).

Servanthood

The foremost symbol for all that Jesus was and did is the cross. It is the symbol of his most radical expression of submission and servanthood. But don't miss the larger truth: The Cross is the climax, the dramatic, final expression of Jesus' self-giving. The climax on Golgotha was a way of life at the center of which was a cross.

One of the most dramatic examples of this cross-bearing way of life was Jesus' action at the Last Supper with his disciples in the upper room. No one was around to perform that common act of a servant for persons coming in off the dusty roads: washing feet. They were meeting in a borrowed room; thus there was no servant or head of the house or anyone to see that the menial task was performed. By washing the disciples' feet, Jesus provided an unforgettable picture of the cross-bearing way of life, the way to which he calls us.

Lest the ongoing meaning of this act be lost in the bafflement of what was happening, Jesus made it evident:

> After washing their feet and taking his garments again, he sat down. "Do you understand," he asked, "what I have done for you? You call me 'Master' and 'Lord,' and rightly so, for that is what I am. Then if I, your Lord and Master, have washed your feet, you also ought to wash one another's feet. I have set you an example: you are to do as I have done for you." (John 13:12-15 NEB)

It's a picture of and a call to the cross-bearing way of life, the life of a servant.

Not only does Jesus call us to the life-style of a servant, but he also gives us life through our obedient response: "Anyone who finds his life will lose it; anyone who loses his life for my sake will find it" (Matthew 10:39 JB). To get the full impact of this, we must note that there is a vast difference between the way most of us serve and Jesus' call to be a servant.

Most of us stay in control even as we serve. We choose whom, when, where, and how we will serve. We hold the reins. Jesus is calling for something else. He is calling us to be servants. When we make this choice, we give up the right to be in charge. I have discovered in my own life, and have seen it in others, that when we make this choice, we experience great freedom. It's an amazing relief. We become available and vulnerable, and we lose our fear of being stepped on or manipulated or taken advantage of. It is when we choose true servanthood, rather than serving now and then as we please, that Christ lives in us forcefully and we communicate his presence vividly to others.

Compassion

If we had to choose words to describe Jesus, high up on the list of words—if not at the very top—would be the word *compassion*. Compassion is love translated into action. There is a wonderful picture of compassion in the first chapter of Mark's Gospel.

Mark tells the story of Jesus' healing a person with leprosy. In New Testament times, leprosy was one of the most dreaded diseases. Not only physical debilitation, but also mental and emotional pain and anguish were parts of the suffering of the person with leprosy. People with leprosy were forced to live alone and wear special clothing so that others could identify and avoid them. Perhaps the most dismal humiliation of all was the law requiring them to announce their despicable condition: *Unclean! Unclean!* Mark tells of one person with leprosy coming boldly to Jesus, kneeling before him, and appealing, "If you want to, you can make me clean." Then there is packed into one beautiful sentence almost everything Jesus was and was about: "Jesus was filled with pity for him, and stretched out his hand and placed it on the leper, saying, 'Of course, I want to—be clean!'" (Mark 1:40 JBP). That tells it all!

By law, the person with leprosy had no right to even draw near Jesus, much less speak to him. How, we do not know, but this person knew that despite his repulsive disease, his grotesque appearance, Jesus would see him, really see him, and respond to him as a person, not as a maimed, disfigured piece of flesh. Note Jesus' responses: He listened, he looked at him, and he touched him—the three action-responses that no one else would dare make. He had *compassion*.

I could have chosen many other stories from the New Testament that make the same point. But I deliberately share this one to express the truth graphically: If Jesus' ministry goes to the extent of involving him with the poorest of poor people, the ugliest of ugly people, can there be any question about what it means to be "little Christs," Christians? We must move through our days responding in compassion, love translated into action, caring for the persons whose lives intersect ours.

Compassion is one of the most characteristic elements of the life of Christ. The Epistle of James says it clearly:

> If a brother or sister is ill-clad and in lack of daily food, and one of you says to them, "Go in peace, be warmed and filled," without giving them the things needed for the body, what does it profit? . . . You see that a man is justified by works and not by faith alone. . . . For as the body apart from the spirit is dead, so faith apart from works is dead. (James 2:15-16, 24, 26 RSV)

I once heard a story about a little boy in Alabama who had no shoes one winter. One day he was standing on a grate next to a bakery to keep his feet warm. A woman came along, and when she saw the boy, her heart went out to him. She couldn't believe that he was standing there in the cold with no shoes and only a light jacket.

"Where are your shoes, young man?" she asked. He said he didn't have any. So the woman said to him, "Why don't you come with me and let's see what we can do about that?" Then she took him by the hand and led him into a nearby department store. There she bought him a new pair of shoes.

When they came out of the store, the little boy was so excited that he took off running down the street to show his family what he had been given. All of a sudden, he came to a halt, turned around, and walked back to the woman. He thanked her, and then he said, "Ma'am, could I ask you a question? Ma'am, are you God's wife?" The woman smiled and said, "Oh, no, I'm not God's wife, just one of God's children." The little boy replied, "I knew it! I knew it! I just knew you were related!"

Christians are related to Christ; we are his disciples. As such, we look like him in our compassion.

Liberation

Another characteristic element of the life of Christ is liberation. As we noted in a previous chapter, Jesus quoted from the prophet Isaiah when he publicly launched his ministry in the synagogue of his hometown, Nazareth:

> The Spirit of the Lord is upon me,
>   because he has anointed me to bring good news to the poor.
> He has sent me to proclaim release to the captives
>   and recovery of sight to the blind,
>   to let the oppressed go free,
> to proclaim the year of the Lord's favor. (Luke 4:18-19)

It is almost impossible to miss the implication that to be a "little Christ" is to take part in the battles for liberating imprisoned, hungry, and homeless people. That's often a very demanding and painful journey because it is to "participate in the sufferings of God in the world."

Matthew, the author of the first Gospel, goes so far as to say that persons who are agents of worldly liberation and reconciliation, who are engaged in ministry to hungry and oppressed people, but who do not yet know or confess the name of Jesus, nevertheless do meet Christ and suffer with him, and in that fashion they participate in that particular aspect of Christ's saving work—deliverance from the powers of bondage and estrangement. This does not mean the agents of liberation do not need to know and worship Christ personally. Indeed, Jesus extends an invitation to enter *knowingly* into the Kingdom and to *know* the Messiah personally, whom one formerly served without knowing: "Come, . . . inherit the kingdom prepared for you from the foundation of the world" (Matthew 25:34 KJV). Thus, knowing Christ as the liberator from sin and guilt, walking with him as he discloses himself in Scripture, in worship, in Christian fellowship, and in the life of the Church, is part of his liberating and reconciling grace at work in the world.

A zealous street evangelist once asked noted theologian H. Richard Niebuhr if he was saved. Niebuhr is said to have replied, "I *was* saved by what Christ did; I *am being* saved right now; I *shall be* saved when the Kingdom comes." That makes the point that salvation is the ongoing work of our lives being transformed more and more into the likeness of Christ. Theologian and author Gabriel Fackre asserts:

> Salvation is a process launched in the saving events that take place in Jesus Christ. It continues into the present as the Holy Spirit moves to deliver and make whole. It reaches a climax when the enemies of God (sin, evil, and death) ultimately surrender and the friends of God are finally brought together. (Fackre, p. 183)

Liberation is salvation *from* all that limits life, all that condemns persons to oppression, lifelessness, lack of dignity and meaning. As Christians, we participate with Christ in that saving work.

How should a Christian live?

As we have noted, Jesus launched his ministry in Nazareth with these words: "The Spirit of the Lord . . . has anointed me to bring good news to the poor . . . has sent me to proclaim release to the captives." And when Jesus promised his followers the Holy Spirit, he said, "You will receive power when the Holy Spirit has come upon you; and you will be my witnesses" (Acts 1:8). Word and deed go together. There are times when the word is the deed—the only deed we can perform. We must speak, even if we can't act. There also are times when acting is the "word" we speak. Of course, we are most effective when both word and deed are combined.

There is a marvelous statement about the necessity of word and deed in the First Epistle of Peter:

> But even if you do suffer for doing what is right, you are blessed. Do not fear what they fear, and do not be intimidated, but in your hearts sanctify Christ as Lord. Always be ready to make your defense to anyone who demands from you an accounting for the hope that is in you. (1 Peter 3:14-15)

Paul established the linkage between word and deed and how essential both are in teaching the Ephesians about gifts and service in the Church:

> The gifts he gave were that some would be apostles, some prophets, some evangelists, some pastors and teachers, to equip the saints for the work of ministry, for building up the body of Christ, until all of us come to the unity of the faith and of the knowledge of the Son of God, to maturity, to the measure of the full stature of Christ. We must no longer be children, tossed to and fro and blown about by every wind of doctrine, by people's trickery, by their craftiness in deceitful scheming. But speaking the truth in love, we must grow up in every way into him who is the head, into Christ. (Ephesians 4:11-15)

So to be "little Christs" in the world is to proclaim the good news of the gospel in both word and deed. As Christians, we do not choose to become new persons; that is a matter already determined by grace. Christ will make us new creatures. We choose, rather, to get on with being Christian—to proclaim the good news in both word and deed. We immerse ourselves in Christ; that is, we surrender ourselves to his Spirit within and allow his grace to make us in reality the new persons we already are in principle—and we begin to walk as we think Christ would have us walk.

Fruits of the Spirit

Being Christian is a way of living, a way of acting, to be sure; it also is a way of being. The apostle Paul talked a lot about "putting on Christ." He contrasts the "works of the flesh" with the "fruit of the Spirit":

> Now the works of the flesh are obvious: fornication, impurity, licentiousness, idolatry, sorcery, enmities, strife, jealousy, anger, quarrels, dissensions, factions, envy, drunkenness, carousing, and things like these. I am warning you, as I warned you before: those who do such things will not inherit the kingdom of God.

By contrast, the fruit of the Spirit is love, joy, peace, patience, kindness, generosity, faithfulness, gentleness, and self-control. There is no law against such things. (Galatians 5:19-23)

Paul's phrase "of the flesh" indicates that way of life in which we are still focused on our own capacities to make a life for ourselves. Even when this way includes religion, it ends in "sin, evil, and death." Paul contrasts that way of life with life in Christ where the power of the Spirit prevails. We are often tempted to turn back to "the flesh" to try to save ourselves, but as those who have "put on Christ," who "walk in the Spirit," and who know the firstfruits of the power of God's love, we are under no obligation to return to the flesh. Indeed, why would we, for we have found a way of life in Christ that far exceeds the dim counterfeits of what we once knew.

Though it is not an exhaustive list, Paul catalogues the works of the flesh and calls Christians to depend on the Spirit for power to overcome these destructive forces in our lives: fornication, impurity (moral uncleanness), licentiousness, idolatry, and sorcery. Then he lists a whole series of words that describe sin in human relations, the sins of self-assertion and pride that destroy community: enmities, strife, jealousy, anger, quarrels, dissensions, factions, envy, drunkenness, carousing, "and things like these." These passions and actions control us when we try to make a life for ourselves apart from Christ.

Must a Christian keep the Ten Commandments?

It is interesting that there is marked connection between the Ten Commandments and Paul's "works of the flesh." The "law" given by God to Moses has found expression not only in Judaism, Christianity, and other religions but also in non-"religious" cultures and communities that seek a moral and ethical guide for life. The Ten Commandments are the most important and universal precepts in the world. They are the foundation upon which law and morals throughout all the world rest.

The question is often asked, "Must a Christian keep the Ten Commandments?" The answer is yes. However, two words in the question need to be considered: *must* and *keep*. The Christian is called to an exemplary moral life, but Christianity is not a "law-keeping" religion. "Keeping the law" is a "fruit" of the Christian's relationship with God through Christ, not the basis for entering into the relationship or finding favor with the Lord.

Knowing that, the call of Paul for Christians is not to surrender to the "works of the flesh"; and the Ten Commandments deserve our daily attention.

Over against these "works of the flesh," which the Ten Commandments condemn, Paul presents the "fruit of the Spirit" as the marks of the Christian. Again, this catalogue is not exhaustive, but the picture is clear: love, joy, peace, patience, kindness, generosity, faithfulness, gentleness, and self-control. Some Bible scholars have said that love is the fruit of the Spirit and all the rest is the harvest of love actualized in our lives. That may be true because we know that God is love and that Jesus is the incarnation of God's love; therefore, to be "little Christs," we are primarily called to love. The fruit of the Spirit, then, includes characteristics of those who in love have put on Christ.

How can I know I am a Christian?

Some time ago I came across this surprising word in John Wesley's *Journal*:

My friends affirm *I am mad*, because I said 'I was not a Christian a year ago.' I affirm, I am not a Christian now. . . . For a Christian is one who has . . . love, peace, joy. But these I have not. . . .

Though I have given and do give all my goods to feed the poor, I am not a Christian. Though I have endured hardship, though I have in all things denied myself and taken up my cross, I am not a Christian. My works are nothing. . . . I have not the fruits of the Spirit of Christ. Though I have constantly used all the means of grace for twenty years, I am not a Christian. (Wesley, vol. 19, pp. 29-31)

John Wesley, founder of the Methodist Movement, wrote that eight months after the occasion he designated as his conversion to Christianity. After years of struggle, seeking to be Christian in every way, Wesley came to the point about which we talked in the chapter on salvation—justification by grace through faith, or the assurance of Christ's saving grace. He testified concerning that experience: "I felt my heart strangely warmed. I felt I did trust in Christ, Christ alone for salvation, and an assurance was given me that he had taken away *my* sins, even *mine,* and saved *me* from the law of sin and death" (Wesley, vol. 18, p. 250).

We ask, What is going on here? Wesley had sought to be a faithful Christian for years. He had been disciplined in his Christian activity and in his prayer and devotional life. He organized a group of young students at Oxford University in England that was referred to as the Holy Club. That group was disciplined in study, worship, and prayer; the participants were also committed to ministering to poor persons, to visiting prisons, to giving away all their money except what was absolutely essential for them to live.

Wesley had been a rigidly disciplined, "law-keeping" Christian, but that had not satisfied him. With his experience that happened in mid-life, after having been a missionary in America, the added dimension of assurance was given. He discovered the core of the Christian gospel—that we do not save ourselves but are saved by the radical love of God, which we discussed in terms of justification by grace through faith. But even after affirming in such an exciting, certain, and confident way the assurance that had been given him, that his sins had been taken away, and that Christ had saved him from "the law of sin and death," Wesley comes now, eight months later, to say emphatically, "I'm not a Christian!"

It raises the whole question about how we use the word *Christian*. One way we might look at it is to assume that Wesley knew himself to be Christian, in *fact* but not in *feeling*. That is an issue with which we have to deal. But more is going on in Wesley's experience. He knew himself to be a follower of Christ, but he also knew that he was not complete. He rejected, as we have already seen, any notion of salvation that is purely *past tense*. He spoke not simply of "being saved" but of "going on to salvation." Christian *in fact,* and yet he knew himself not to be a Christian. My assumption is that Wesley was confessing what we so often feel—that while we have accepted the salvation of Jesus Christ, while we believe the gospel, and while we are seeking to act out our discipleship as a part of the Body of Christ, still we know how far short we fall in being "little Christs"—in expressing the presence of Christ in the world. We look at a person like Mother Teresa, and we hang our heads in shame.

For sincere disciples, ones who wish to be followers of Christ, that is our constant dilemma: We are never as Christian as we might be or as we are called to be. The Christian life is not a life of instant perfection that we accomplish or that is given us in a moment. It is not a place to which we arrive; it is a journey. John Wesley talked about it in terms of going on to salvation, to "perfection in love."

I think it is helpful to distinguish between the word *Christian* as a noun and as an adjective. To be *a* Christian (noun) is to be one who professes the Christian faith and has begun the journey. To be Christian (adjective)—to be a *Christian person*—is to be one whose life reflects the life of Christ. That means that one can grow as a Christian and that not all Christians are at the same place in their journeys.

Surely not all of us are at the same place as Mother Teresa. Part of the way we know this is that Mother Teresa would be the last to concern herself with such comparisons—she is too busy serving the Christ hidden in her neighbor. There comes a point in our Christian pilgrimage when doctrine and belief cease to be central. Jesus made that very clear when he was debating with the Jews. They were astonished at his teaching and wondered about how he had such learning—being a carpenter and, according to them, "never been taught." In response to their astonished questioning, Jesus said, "My teaching is not mine but his who sent me. Anyone who resolves to do the will of God will know whether the teaching is from God or whether I am speaking on my own" (John 7:16-17). That's an interesting twist. Jesus was saying, "Any person who does the will of God will know the truth—the teaching of God." So there is a sense in which to understand and to grow as Christians is not a matter of the intellect but a matter of being willing to follow Jesus.

Someone has defined a *saint* as "one in whom Christ is felt to live again." That really is a definition of any of us who would be truly and fully Christian. The whole meaning of living the Christian life is continuing the life of Christ, replicating that life in the world. This happens through the power of the Holy Spirit and obedience—our seeking to be and do everything Christ calls us to be and do, which means that what Christ has been and done for us, we must be and do for others. Clearly this is a journey that continues into eternity.

One of the most Christlike persons I know is Pauline Hord, an older member of a congregation I served. Here is her story as I told it in *Congregational Evangelism*:

> Pauline is a remarkable woman. She is the most unique blending of prayer and personal piety, with servant ministry and social concern, I know. . . .
>
> Pauline's current passion is literacy and prison ministry. . . . Pauline is working with our public schools, training teachers in a new literacy method. She gives three days a week, four or five hours a day, to teaching this new method of literacy in model programs.

But, also, once a week she drives over a hundred miles one way to Parchman State Prison down in Mississippi, to teach prisoners to read and write. Along with this, she ministers to them in a more encompassing way as she shares her love and faith, and witnesses to the power of the gospel. . . .

Sometime ago, President George Bush started a program in the United States called "Points of Light." He was calling for citizens to exercise positive and creative influence and service in the areas where they lived. In the different cities and communities of America, people were recognized for being "points of light." I nominated Pauline Hord for that honor, and she was written up in our daily newspaper.

. . . President Bush came to Memphis. He wanted to honor the seven most outstanding "points of light" in our city—the people who had done the most for the sake of humankind. Pauline Hord was one of those selected. The President invited these seven to have lunch with him when he came for his visit to Memphis.

But, he made a mistake. He set the luncheon on a Wednesday. That's the day Pauline spends at Parchman Prison in Mississippi, teaching prisoners to read and write, and witnessing to them of the love of Christ. She would not give that up to have lunch with the President. (Dunnam, *Congregational Evangelism*, pp. 29-30)

Pauline is both a Christian (noun) and Christian (adjective). To know her is to catch a concrete vision of what it means to live as a Christian.

Summary

Christians are "little Christs." Being Christian is being Christ in the world. What Christ has been and done for us, as Christians we must be and do for the world. We must live as Christ in our daily relationships.

The most effective way of communicating Christ's presence to others is loving service. As servants, compassion and liberation characterize our lives. We proclaim the good news in word and deed.

Our way of life, our sense of morality, and our desire to be clear reflections of Christ in terms of relationship and the shape of character indicate how far along we are in our Christian pilgrimage and to what degree the Holy Spirit is shaping our lives into the likeness of Christ.

CHAPTER SEVEN

THE RESURRECTION, ETERNAL LIFE, AND THE KINGDOM OF GOD

What is the Resurrection, and what significance does it have for my life?

Natalie Sleeth has given us one of the most popular hymns written during the past twenty-five years. It is titled "Hymn of Promise." The last two lines of the hymn will give you the core message:

> In our death, a resurrection; at the last, a victory,
> unrevealed until its season, something God alone can see.

She wrote the hymn for her husband, the late Ronald Sleeth, who was professor of preaching at the Iliff School of Theology. From date of diagnosis of a malignancy to death were just twenty-one days, and Natalie wrote that hymn for him before he died.

A personal friend of the Sleeths told me a moving story. For several years Natalie had battled multiple sclerosis, which ultimately took her life. Before she died she wrote a beautiful statement for her grandchildren in which she told of how she began to realize that she was growing older and that her body was beginning to wear out. She talked to God about the situation and asked God to help her. God heard her and said, "My child, when I made the world and filled it with people, I had a plan. I wanted my people to have life for as long as they could, but not forever because then my world would be too full with no room for anybody. I planned it so that when it was time to leave the earth, my people would come and live with me in heaven where there is no pain or sadness or sickness or anything bad."

Natalie said softly to God, "Is my time to come and live with you getting closer?" And God said, "Yes, but be not afraid for I will always be with you and I will always take care of you." Natalie said to God, "But I will miss my family and my friends, and they will miss me!" And God said, "Yes, but I will comfort them and turn their tears into joy and they will remember you with happiness and be glad of your life among them."

Slowly Natalie began the journey to heaven and day by day drew nearer to God. In the distance she could see light and hear beautiful music and feel happiness she had never known before, and as she moved toward the gates and into the house of God, she said to herself with great joy in her heart, "That's good! That's good!"

Natalie Sleeth claimed one of the central truths of the Christian faith—the promise that death is not the end. The resurrection of Christ gives credence to his claim, "Because I live, you will live also" (John 14:19 RSV). The heartbeat of the gospel is the death and resurrection of Jesus. Natalie Sleeth experienced the meaning and hope of this powerful reality that Jesus died but was raised by God and offers us the same glorious possibility.

The driving power behind the Christian faith is the resurrection of Jesus. In the beginning, as the faith was being experienced, expressed, and celebrated in community, to be an apostle meant that you were an eyewitness to the Resurrection. The four Gospels in the New Testament (Matthew, Mark, Luke, and John) provide a picture of Jesus that could have been shared only by those who had experienced him as the risen Lord.

The Resurrection was the theme of every Christian sermon. It was the dominating motive behind every act of Christian evangelism. One person wrote:

> Not one line of the New Testament was written . . . not one sentence was penned apart from the conviction that He of whom these things were being written had conquered death and was alive forever. . . . The one and only God the apostles worshipped was the God of the resurrection. The one and only Gospel they were commissioned to preach was the overpowering, magnificent Good News of the resurrection. (Stuart, p. 105)

Paul, the writer of the major part of the New Testament, said that our faith, our hope, and our preaching are all in vain if there is no Resurrection (1 Corinthians 15:14).

Here are some of the ways the significance of the Resurrection is expressed in the New Testament:

> I am come that [you] might have life, and that [you] might have it more abundantly. (John 10:10 KJV)

> Because I live, ye shall live also. (John 14:19 KJV)

> This is eternal life: to know thee who alone art truly God, and Jesus whom thou hast sent. (John 17:3 NEB)

> God gave us eternal life, and this life is in his Son. Whoever has the Son has life; whoever does not have the Son of God does not have life. (1 John 5:11-12)

> If any one is in Christ, he is a new creation; the old has passed away, behold, the new has come. (2 Corinthians 5:17 RSV)

> Then I saw a new heaven and a new earth; for the first heaven and the first earth had passed away. . . . And I heard a loud voice from the throne saying, "See, the home of God is among mortals . . . for the first things have passed away. . . . See, I am making all things new." (Revelation 21:1, 3, 4, 5)

To be sure, the Resurrection is central to the Christian gospel. The Christian gospel is the proclamation of an event, the event of Jesus Christ. In the Christian view of reality, Jesus is final. He is the revelation of God and the revelation of humanity. In Jesus Christ, God has come to us, has been present in our midst, and has made known his love. Prodigal persons, a long way from the Father's house—some having forgotten where the house is, some even having forgotten that there is a Father—have been brought home. At least the road back has been opened. Our desire to be connected with God, a desire that we can never achieve on our own, has been established from the other side: "In Christ God was reconciling the world to himself" (2 Corinthians 5:19).

The New Testament writers were preaching the Resurrection as a fact. Renowned preacher Samuel Shoemaker once said:

> The Church and the Bible do not explain the resurrection: They are explained by it, and they start with it. There would have been no Church and no Bible unless there had first been the fact of the resurrection. On Good Friday, Jesus died, an apparent failure. His friends scattered, and His movement stopped; but on Easter He rose again from the dead, His friends re-assembled, and His movement started up again, never to stop. The resurrection explains these things. It is an event of the same order of the Creation itself. It inaugurates a new creation. (Dunnam, *That's What the Man Said*, p. 105)

Yet the Christian gospel is more than the proclamation of an event; it is an invitation to an encounter—an encounter with Christ. The resurrection of Jesus does not simply mean that Jesus is alive. It means that Jesus is alive *here* and *now, among us.* He gives the promise: "Because I live, ye shall live also" (John 14:19 KJV). The early followers of Christ preached the Resurrection as a fact, and they lived it as an experience. They had received a Kingdom that could not be shaken, a life that could not be snuffed out by death. That is the reason that, through the years, Christians have been willing to bear all sorts of burdens, make all sorts of sacrifices, take all sorts of risks to proclaim the gospel. That's the reason that countless persons have been willing to literally die for the cause of Jesus Christ.

Victory Over Death

Let's pursue the implications of the fact of the Resurrection for our lives. The resurrection of Jesus confronts human-kind's most ominous enemy, death, and wins. A long time ago, Job, a tragic figure in the Old Testament who deals profoundly with faithfulness to God in the presence of evil, pain, and suffering, introduced a searching question with a little word *if*: "If mortals die, will they live again?" (Job 14:14).

There is no *if* about death. Job knew that. Even when he said that word, he was wrestling with the fact of his death. The question is more accurately put, "*When* a person dies, shall he or she live again?" Death is inevitable, and nowhere is the fact put more starkly than by the writer of the Epistle to the Hebrews: "It is appointed for mortals to die once, and after that the judgment" (Hebrews 9:27).

Yet, in the Christian faith and experience, death is not the victor, and death is not the end. Someone has put it crypti-cally: The difference between life and death is more than a tombstone—the difference is Jesus Christ. Jesus said, "I am the resurrection and the life. Those who believe in me, even though they die, will live, and everyone who lives and be-lieves in me will never die" (John 11:25-26). Through his resurrection, Jesus conquered death.

Paul said that "Christ [has] abolished death" (2 Timothy 1:10), death being "the last enemy" (1 Corinthians 15:26). This is the way he writes about it:

Listen, I will tell you a mystery! We will not all die, but we will all be changed, in a moment, in the twinkling of an eye, at the last trumpet. For the trumpet will sound, and the dead will be raised imperishable, and we will be changed. For this perishable body must put on imperishability, and this mortal body must put on immortality. When this perishable body puts on imperishability, and this mortal body puts on immortality, then the saying that is written will be fulfilled:

"Death has been swallowed up in victory."
"Where, O death, is your victory?
  Where, O death, is your sting?"
The sting of death is sin, and the power of sin is the law. But thanks be to God, who gives us the victory through our Lord Jesus Christ. (1 Corinthians 15:54*d*-57)

Paul is talking not only about physical death but also about spiritual death. Spiritual death is the result of sin, which separates us from God. We talked about this in chapter 3. If we refuse the saving grace of Christ and allow sin to reign in our lives, then spiritual death, separation from God, is certain.

Bible commentator Alexander Maclaren has put it in an incisive way:

It is not so much that physical fact (of death) with its accompaniments which Paul is thinking about when he says that "sin reigns in death," as it is that solemn truth which he is always reiterating, and which I pray you, dear friends, to lay to heart, that whatever activity there may be in the life of a man who has rent himself away from dependence upon God—however vigorous his brain, however active his hand, however full-charged with other interests his life, in the very depths of it, it is a living death, and the right name for it is death. So this is sin's gift—that over our whole nature there come mortality and decay, and that they who live as her subjects—(the subjects of sin)—are dead—[even while they live]. (Maclaren, p. 111)

In both cases—physical and spiritual death—the resurrection of Jesus comes into play. Death has been abolished by Jesus Christ.

The Promise of Eternal Life

In Jesus, God completed his mighty work of incarnation and redemption. The promise of Jesus had the proof of his very life: "I am the resurrection and the life. Those who believe in me, even though they die, will live, and everyone who lives and believes in me will never die" (John 11:25-26). The answer to physical and spiritual death is the resurrected and living Christ.

Jesus' resurrection and his promise of eternal life speak to our threatened identity, our feelings of worthlessness, our lack of self-value and self-esteem. The raging materialism of our day tends to reduce us to numbers.

To our threatened identity, to our lack of confidence and feeling about value and worth, the promise of resurrection speaks a powerful word. Jesus is saying to us: You are important, so important that I gave my life for you, so important that I offer you eternal life.

Because Jesus is the resurrection and the life, we can sustain a vision of hope. Hope is of the essence of eternal life; it is one of those things that is eternal, that endures when all else fails (1 Corinthians 13).

Even before Jesus' resurrection, God planted a vision of hope in the minds and hearts of his people. One chapter of the history of God's people is a dramatic witness. Moses and Joshua were leading the Israelites out of captivity. When they came near the promised land, the people were in the choking grip of negative thinking. They had a defeatist mentality and complained about everything: The food was not good, and the accommodations were worse. They were frightened of the future, and they wallowed in despair. They even accused Moses and Joshua of a subversive plot to kill them. When they surveyed the land God had promised them, they laid on themselves the ultimate put-down—they saw themselves as grasshoppers and their enemies as giants.

Moses grew weary of their complaining antagonism, and Joshua was fed up. Even God cried out, "How long shall this wicked congregation complain against me?" (Numbers 14:27). To add to the despair and hopelessness, Moses died.

Then an amazing thing happened. The first chapter of Joshua opens with this word: "After the death of Moses the servant of the LORD, the LORD said to Joshua the son of Nun, Moses' minister, "My servant Moses is dead. Now proceed to cross the Jordan, you and all this people, into the land that I am giving to them" (Joshua 1:1-2).

For forty years the people of Israel had depended on Moses. He was a great leader, the great emancipator. Now he was dead, and Joshua was thrust into leadership. He and the people were discouraged and depressed. But God said, "Arise! Get Up! Be done with this hopelessness; go over into Jordan, you and all the people, into the land which I am giving them" (paraphrase).

That fired hope, and the defeated, discouraged people were transformed. They had no military training because they were the descendants of slaves; yet, fortified with faith and hope, they moved into a land occupied by people with vastly superior weapons and fortified cities, and they conquered it.

How did it happen? What was their secret? They took God at his promise. And what was that promise? Read Joshua 1:5-6:

> No one shall be able to stand against you all the days of your life. As I was with Moses, so I will be with you; I will not fail you or forsake you. Be strong and courageous; for you shall put this people in possession of the land that I swore to their ancestors to give them.

Any number of stories dramatize the vision of hope that God planted in the minds and hearts of his people. I rehearse this one to underscore again the continuing revelation and the movement of salvation history; also, I use it because Jesus is our Joshua. *Joshua* is the Hebrew name for Jesus. Jesus is the fulfillment of the law of Moses, but more. As God allowed

Joshua to enter the land of promise, Jesus leads us to the ultimate Promised Land.

Before the Resurrection, hope depended on God breaking into human history in an episodic sort of way. But now, in the Resurrection, there is a once-and-for-all event. Hope has been given the substance of life itself. For that reason Paul argues forcefully that the Resurrection was the hinge issue of the Christian faith: "If Christ has not been raised, your faith is futile and you are still in your sins. . . . If for this life only we have hoped in Christ, we are of all people most to be pitied" (1 Corinthians 15:17, 19).

Hope, for Christians, is not hoping in the normal sense of the word; it is not wishful thinking. It is the very substance of faith that gives us our greatest certainty. I like that word from the Epistle to the Hebrews: "But we are not among those who shrink back and so are lost, but among those who have faith and so are saved" (Hebrews 10:39).

Perhaps the most powerful implication of the Resurrection for everyday living is this: We are not victims either of circumstance or of death. The promise of the Resurrection and our hope for eternal life make us victors.

Huber Matos was a teacher and a journalist who was imprisoned by Castro in 1959 when Castro sought to destroy the church in Cuba. Many Christian leaders and those who courageously stood for freedom were imprisoned. In a letter, smuggled out of a prison in Havana, to his wife and children, Matos said, "I know that I will die in prison. I am sad not to see you again, but I am at peace. They have swords, but we have songs."

Consider the difference between Matos and a young woman of whom I read. She was intelligent and fabulously wealthy. With energy and shrewdness, she had amassed a fortune in the world of investments. She seemed to have it all, but she was lacking something, like the rich young ruler who went to Jesus because of his inner emptiness. The young woman drove her silver Mercedes convertible to a hotel, checked in, and then checked out for good. She died of a drug overdose, leaving a note that read: "I'm tired of clapping with one hand."

That young woman did not know the peace of Matos; she did not have the song of Matos. She did not know Jesus, who is the resurrection and the life.

The gift of eternal life enables us to be victors over circumstances and death.

What does it mean to have eternal life?

A minister friend told a story of a couple who had been married for twelve years when the woman was stricken with cancer. Medically, the situation seemed hopeless. But each day in the hospital the couple read together the stories of how Jesus healed so many people in his earthly ministry.

As they read, their despair turned to hope, and they began praying together earnestly, knowing that the Lord who loved her would also heal her. But she was not healed. After her death, her husband wrote a letter to his friends describing how their faith brought them through the long days of suffering. Even to the end their trust never wavered. They believed that God's way is perfect, and that there is a greater miracle even than healing: resurrection.

There is nothing distinctively Christian about belief in immortality; many religions—and many people with little or no religion—believe in the survival of the soul, the Greek philosophy that regards immortality as an inherent attribute of the human spirit. When we address the issue as Christians, we either have to talk about Christian immortality or restrict ourselves to using the phrase "eternal life." Christian immortality, or eternal life, is different from the natural wish for survival. Our faith in personal immortality is anchored in the resurrection of Jesus. We rely on Jesus' promise: "Because I live, ye shall live also."

As Christians, we believe in the resurrection of the body

and the life everlasting. Christianity does not go along with the Greek philosophy of drawing a sharp distinction between soul and body. We look upon a human being as an integrated whole. So, when we say that we believe in the resurrection of the body, we are not saying that our physical bodies as such will be restored after death. Paul makes that very clear: "Flesh and blood cannot inherit the kingdom of God" (1 Corinthians 15:50). The "body" to which the Bible refers is spiritual rather than physical, but the point is this: We persons who have received the gift of eternal life from Christ will maintain our identities, including our self-awareness and the ability to communicate in some fashion.

Paul does declare that there is a "spiritual body" (1 Corinthians 15:44). See those two words together: not a spirit only, but a "spiritual body." Of course it's not like the natural body, but it must be more than pure spirit can be. We understand it best, I think, as we think about the survival of the whole personality—not just individuality, not just soul, but the whole self with something that corresponds to the body of our present time that will be aware and can communicate.

Though we may not be able to explain the resurrection of the body and the life everlasting, we can affirm this remarkable, life-changing promise of Jesus: "I am the resurrection and the life. Those who believe in me, even though they die, will live, and everyone who lives and believes in me will never die" (John 11:25-26). The mystery of that is profound, and we will have to live with that mystery until the full experience comes.

What is heaven like?

There was a southern California courier service that, for a season at least, did a brisk business with something called Heaven's Union. The company offered to deliver messages to loved ones in heaven via persons who were terminally ill. The charge was $40 for fifty words or less; $60 for one hundred words. They even had a High Priority service for $125, which delivered the messages through three separate couriers—I suppose in the event that your designated recipient was hard to find!

That company did business because of our insatiable curiosity about the afterlife. We Christians, and others, want to know what heaven is like. In the Bible and in our faith tradition, we have an abundance of promises but an economy of detail. From the nature of God as we have seen him in Jesus Christ, and from the promises of Scripture, we can surmise in a trustful way that heaven will be an experience of re-creation. John, the writer of the Revelation, received a vision in which Christ said, "See, I am making all things new" (Revelation 21:5). That harmonizes with all we believe. So, John heard a loud voice saying:

> See, the home of God is
>   among mortals.
> He will dwell with them as
>   their God;
> they will be his peoples,
> and God himself will be with
>   them;
> he will wipe every tear from
>   their eyes.
> Death will be no more;
> mourning and crying and pain
>   will be no more,
> for the first things have passed
>   away. (Revelation 21:3-4)

In heaven, all that we are will be renewed and/or recreated. Heaven will be an experience of reunion. We have already discussed the fact that persons who have received the gift of eternal life from Christ will maintain their identities, including self-awareness and the ability to communicate in some fashion. It follows that heaven, then, is an experience of reunion.

As I write this, my mother is making a very slow recovery from a stroke. She is eighty-eight, and the possibility of full recovery looks very dim. One of my most painful experiences is to visit her and not be known. Her mind comes and goes, and sometimes she simply doesn't know who I am. When she does know, she always wants those around to know I'm her "baby" (the youngest in the family) and that I'm also the preacher for which she prayed throughout the rearing of her five children.

In the reunion of heaven, Mamma will know me all the time; there will be no coming and going of her mind. She will be healed and renewed, and we will know and love.

Acclaimed author Henri Nouwen offered a wonderful metaphor to illustrate this point. He said that every time he travels anywhere in the world and lands at some strange airport, he has a fantasy that someone will be there who will say, "Hey, Henri! Welcome!" It will be somebody who knows him and who will welcome him with an embrace and a smile. Each time he waits for the voice, and each time he is disappointed. But then he says to himself, *It's all right. When I get home, my friends or family will be there.* Nevertheless, the fantasy persists. Every time he lands at a new airport he waits for the "Hey, Henri! Over here! How are you? Glad to see you!" Each time he is disappointed, but then he remembers that when he arrives back home, his friends and his family will be there.

Then he said that heaven will be like that. God will be there, and all his friends and family who have died. And when they see him, they will say, "Hey, Henri! Glad to see you! How was it? Let's see your slides'."

Recognition and reunion—yes; perhaps in a new dimension that we don't yet know but real.

Recognition and reunion—and *rejoicing*. Though I haven't sung it in years, I still remember most of the words of "When We All Get to Heaven," a gospel song we sang in the little country church of my growing-up years:

Sing the wondrous love of Jesus;
sing his mercy and his grace.
In the mansions bright and blessed
he'll prepare for us a place.

When we all get to heaven,
what a day of rejoicing that will be!
When we all see Jesus,
we'll sing and shout the victory!

While we walk the pilgrim pathway,
clouds will overspread the sky;
but when traveling days are over,
not a shadow, not a sigh.

Refrain

Let us then be true and faithful,
trusting, serving every day;
just one glimpse of him in glory
will the toils of life repay.

Refrain

Onward to the prize before us!
Soon his beauty we'll behold;
soon the pearly gates will open;
we shall tread the streets of gold.

Refrain

That congregation knew that if heaven was real, if the promise of eternal life had integrity, *rejoicing* was the order of the day, *now* and *then*. Heaven is where God, Jesus, and the Holy Spirit dwell as one and wait to welcome us into that heavenly abode.

To claim that we know *much* about heaven is overstating the case. But the little we know is enough to keep our hearts happy and hopeful.

What is the kingdom of God, and when will it come?

Christians the world over pray what we've come to call the Lord's Prayer. In this prayer we make the petition, "Thy kingdom come. Thy will be done in earth, as it is in heaven." It is obvious that this prayer is yet to be answered. Things are not as they should be; life is certainly not as God intended it to be. There is graphic confirmation of this in a word and picture essay titled "Corridors of Agony" in *Time* (May 17, 1992).

It is the story of children caught in the web of abuse. The article explains how the problems of these children are compounded because of the hopeless jungle of our juvenile courts. Several sad stories are told.

There is Antwan, age ten. His mother warned him about the drug dealers who hung around the playground where he spent hours each day. A mother's warnings were no match for threats by street thugs, though. The drug dealers knew how to shield themselves from the law. They kept a small child nearby when they were dealing drugs. If the police closed in, they would be all right because they hid the drugs on the child. When the police moved in, they found vials of narcotics stuffed in Antwan's socks.

The essay tells about Emily, age six, and her sister, age ten, victims of incest by their father. They were sexually abused in the bedroom while their mother was cooking dinner. The picture is a heartbreaking one: Emily clings to a doll that plays "It's a Small World After All."

There are tragic stories of other children. To close the essay, the writer returns to Antwan's apartment—the ten-year-old with drugs stuffed in his socks. He has been placed in a special program that offers him at least a glimmer of a better life. The writer tells how his mother unscrews the light bulb from the kitchen socket and screws it into the fixture in the living room ceiling. It is the only light bulb they have. Its harsh glow illuminates a poster on a far wall of a young black boy crying. The caption at the bottom reads: "He will wipe away all tears from their eyes, and there shall be no more death, nor sorrow, nor crying, nor pain. All of that has gone forever."

I know nothing of the writer's Christian commitment or religious understanding. Whether intentional or not, the writer gives a convincing picture of how far we are now from the Kingdom, and yet, how poignantly powerful is the promise of the Kingdom. The caption on the poster comes from John's vision of the coming Kingdom, a portion of which I quoted earlier:

> Then I saw a new heaven and a new earth; for the first heaven and the first earth had passed away, and the sea was no more. And I saw the holy city, the new Jerusalem, coming down out of heaven from God, prepared as a bride adorned for her husband. And I heard a loud voice from the throne saying,
> "See, the home of God is among mortals.
> He will dwell with them as their God;
> they will be his peoples,
> and God himself will be with them;
> he will wipe every tear from their eyes.
> Death will be no more;
> mourning and crying and pain will be no more,
> for the first things have passed away."
> And the one who was seated on the throne said, "See, I am making all things new." (Revelation 21:1-5*a*)

John foresees the day when hope reaches fulfillment and our prayers are answered: God's will is done on earth and in heaven. The wages of sin and evil are death. Liberation from the destruction of these enemies is everlasting life, which will be completed in God's finished work, the Kingdom. That life and Kingdom are not yet complete but have begun. There is the coming Kingdom, when history will be brought to a close and God's reign will be established over all creation. But don't miss the fact: there also is the Kingdom *now*.

John is the New Testament writer who writes most about eternal life. In the first three Gospels, Matthew, Mark, and Luke, Jesus centers his message on the Kingdom that "has come near." The two, *eternal life* in John's Gospel and *the Kingdom* in the other Gospels, are ways of talking about God's purpose in history. The structure of both eternal life and the kingdom of God in the New Testament involves an "already" and a "not yet." There Jesus speaks of the Kingdom "in your midst" and the Kingdom "yet to come." They are the same Kingdom—the rule of God— only differentiated by degree of realization. And as already indicated, eternal life is a gift that we receive now, already abiding in those who believe, but also something yet to come.

The Kingdom—and eternal life—is not simply a place or time for which Christians hope, look, or move in the future; it is *now*—a *way of life* that grows deeper as we "go on to salvation." Israel hoped for and at times glimpsed the Kingdom. Jesus is the firstfruits of the Kingdom and inaugurates a level of intimacy that fulfills the promise Israel hoped for. Persons experienced this hope and anticipation in what Paul calls the "fruit of the Spirit," which Jesus summed up in the command to love God, neighbor, and self.

It all fits together. The kingdom of God is the will, rule, and reign of God, and love is at the center. So Paul declares "faith, hope, and love" endure. They are eternal: We have them now, we receive them in the next world, so the Kingdom is "already" and "not yet come."

How are we to live in the meantime?

There is a sense in which the film *Driving Miss Daisy* is a part of the gospel in capsule form. In the beginning, the strong-willed and opinionated Miss Daisy regards with disdain the driver her son has hired to drive her car and take her places. She derides and belittles him, all of which he receives with equanimity. She doesn't trust him, but over the years he tolerates and absorbs her willful stubbornness. Her ingrained, insensitive prejudice is transformed by the gentle man who gradually becomes her trusted companion and friend.

The movie ends with a powerful witness. Two elderly people—the wealthy educated Jewish woman, now in a nursing home, almost unable to even feed herself, and the wise but uneducated black man who had been her chauffeur—share a friendship and an understanding that are truly spiritual gifts. The camera focuses for a mind-gripping moment on two hands—the strong black hand of the chauffeur and the bony frail white hand of Miss Daisy in solid grasp. It's a moment of transparent truth, suggesting the shalom of the Kingdom.

Until the Kingdom comes fully, how do we live in the meantime? We seek to live into the Kingdom, to move farther up and farther into the heavenly order that we have already tasted in this life. Though it may seem impossible in our sinful world to realize the ideal of justice, mercy, reconciliation, and peace, though the healing of the nations and our wounded earth has not been realized, that does not excuse us from doing justice and exercising love and compassion now. Nor is it convincing evidence that justice and peace are not growing now—like wheat among weeds, both in our individual lives and in our life together.

Consider again the *Time* article. Do we think we can talk about justice to Antwan and Emily? "There is no justice," they would say, and in this experience they are right. But do we leave it there? Are we going to become cynical and/or hopeless? Are we going to refuse to show mercy and act justly because it's only a drop in the bucket—or maybe only a few raindrops on the vast desert of injustice and violence?

As Christians, we do not hunker down in retreat or wring our hands in despair, no matter what is going on in the world. We have only two legitimate positions—on our knees in prayer, saying, "Lord, have mercy on me, a sinner," or on our feet, standing erect, saying, "Here am I, Lord, send me." Despair paralyzes. Hope mobilizes. Christians have hope.

The power of the Kingdom (of eternal life, of faith, hope, and love) is the power that overcomes and endures even in the face of evil and suffering. It endures both by opposing and exposing evil and by staying *alive* in suffering. In this light, the hope of eternal life is not a pie-in-the-sky projection to help people ignore their suffering. Rather, this hope is precisely what makes it possible for them to name the evil and challenge it, to face even death with faith that is stronger than fear. This hope also enables those who may not be oppressed to learn from poor and suffering people what it means to have faith: quit oppressing; cease passively watching; get into eternal life now, for faith, hope, and love endure, not because we want them to, but because they are Kingdom forces stronger than fear, cynicism, despair, and violence.

In his resurrection, Jesus Christ has conquered death and has given us a guarantee of life everlasting and a Kingdom that will know no end, a Kingdom where nothing can separate us from the love of God in Christ Jesus (Romans 8:38-39). Everything that touches our fear and anxiety—from growing older to not having enough food, from the specter of random crime and violence to short tempers that fly when our comfort zone is invaded—has its roots in our fear of death, the ultimate enemy. This death has a thousand faces. Because Jesus endured to the ultimate extent his undeserved death, and because God raised him, to live in the power of the Resurrection and eternity under God's rule is to lose our fear of death, and to trust God to save us now and forever.

So, Christians do not separate the Kingdom now from the Kingdom that is to come. Our eternal life *has begun*. We are Kingdom people who live God's vision of shalom and invite others to participate with us. In one of Charles Wesley's most popular hymns, "O for a Thousand Tongues to Sing," he expresses the fact of the Kingdom now, "heaven below":

> In Christ, your head, you then shall know,
> shall feel your sins forgiven;

anticipate your heaven below,
and own that love is heaven.

When I think of the Kingdom, and the triumph of the Kingdom now and in the future, I remember an experience I had several years ago. My wife, Jerry, and I visited churches in what was then Czechoslovakia. I was deeply moved by that experience. There are not many members, but they are committed Christians. One pastor who came to spend the day with us in a seminar spent more than one-half his monthly salary to buy the gasoline to come to the meeting. As I looked at the pastors and laypersons, I saw in them a people who were filled with great hope. But no wonder! Until November 1989, every church in Czechoslovakia was severely restricted by the Communist government. Christians could not evangelize. They had to be careful about how they spoke in public. They could post no public notices on their church buildings. No sign could be erected outside their churches. They could make no public declarations. They could not even ring their church bells.

Then in November 1989, a group of students confronted a group of young soldiers, and that catalyst brought the revolution against the government out in the open and to full flower. Everybody took to the streets, and the old Communist regime knew that it was over.

Christians there told us the story. It was decided that on November 27 at noon, everybody in the country would walk out of homes, businesses, offices, factories, or fields. Everybody would simply walk out into the streets at noon. Every bell in every church in Czechoslovakia would be rung at noon. And when that day and time came, bells that had been silent for forty-five years began to ring. It was electric. Everybody knew that something new had come.

Dr. Vilem Schneeberger, one of the pastors, said that for the first time they were able to put a sign out in front of their church in Prague. On the sign were written four words: "The Lamb Has Won."

What a truth! What a victory! What a sign of the Kingdom! *The Lamb has won!* Not the bear, but the Lamb! Not the tiger, but the Lamb! Not the lion, but the Lamb!

We can believe it. One day "every knee should bend . . . and every tongue . . . confess that Jesus Christ is Lord, to the glory of God the Father" (Philippians 2:10-11). So be it! Hallelujah!

Summary

The Resurrection, eternal life, and the kingdom of God go together. The resurrection of Jesus is the driving power behind the Christian faith. The fact of the Resurrection confirms Jesus' promise of eternal life for all those who live and believe in him.

Though heaven is our destination beyond death, eternal life is an experience into which we enter now. Death as the enemy has been conquered—both physical and spiritual death. In the Resurrection, God completes his mighty work of incarnation and redemption.

The gift of eternal life enlivens us to overcome our threatened identity, our lack of confidence about our value and self-worth. It enables us to sustain a vision of hope and not become victims either of circumstance or death.

We live in hope for the coming of the Kingdom when God's reign will be established over all creation. Until that time, we live as though the Kingdom has already come; thus we seek to approximate in this earthly order what already exists in the heavenly order. Though the Kingdom has not yet fully come, we are not excused from doing justice and exercising love and mercy now.

We live in hope, empowered by the fact that in his resurrection Jesus conquered death, has guaranteed us eternal life, and gives us a Kingdom that will know no end—a Kingdom where nothing can separate us from the love of God in Christ Jesus.

BIBLIOGRAPHY

Angelou, Maya. *I Know Why the Caged Bird Sings.* New York: Bantam, 1970.

Barclay, William. *Daily Study Bible: The Letter to the Galatians and Ephesians.* Edinburgh: Saint Andrew Press, 1954.

Brown, Robert McAfee. "Thinking About God." *Christianity and Crisis,* May 27, 1991.

Cassels, Louis. *Christian Primer.* New York: Doubleday, 1964.

Dionysius the Areopagite. Trans. C. E. Rolt. London: SPCK, 1979.

Dunnam, Maxie. *Congregational Evangelism.* Nashville: Discipleship Resources, 1992.

———. *That's What the Man Said.* Nashville: Upper Room, 1989.

Fackre, Gabriel. *The Christian Story.* Grand Rapids, Mich.: Eerdmans, 1978.

Friesen, Garry, and J. Robin Maxson. *Decision Making and the Will of God.* Lemon Grove, Calif.: Questar, 1983.

Green, Michael. *Who Is This Jesus?* Nashville: Thomas Nelson, 1990.

Jennings, Theodore W., Jr. *Loyalty to God.* Nashville: Abingdon, 1992.

Lewis, C. S. *Mere Christianity.* New York: Macmillan, 1943.

Maclaren, Alexander. *Expositions of Holy Scripture.* Vol. 12. Grand Rapids, Mich.: Baker, 1975.

Muggeridge, Malcolm. *Jesus: The Man Who Lives.* New York: Harper and Row, 1975.

Schell, Orvil. *In the People's Republic.* New York: Random House, 1977.

Stuart, James S. *A Faith to Proclaim.* New York: Charles Scribner & Sons, 1953.

ten Boom, Corrie. *The Hiding Place.* Uhrichsville, Ohio: Barbour and Co., 1971.

Wesley, John. *The Works of John Wesley.* Vols. 18 and 19. Nashville: Abingdon Press, 1988 and 1990.

Suggestions for Leading a Study of *This Is Christianity*

This Is Christianity offers a basic understanding of the Christian faith. As a discussion leader, you have the opportunity to help others obtain the answers they are seeking on their spiritual journey. The conversations in your group may cover a variety of topics as together you ask questions and seek answers. Here are some thoughts on how to best facilitate this process.

1. Read the entire book before your first group meeting. This will provide you with an overview of the material and will better equip you as a leader. You may want to use a highlighter to designate important points.

2. Distribute the book to participants before the first meeting and request they come having read the first chapter. You may want to limit the size of your group to increase participation.

3. Begin each session by reviewing the main points using the chapter summary in this leader's guide. You also may want to read aloud the author's summary at the end of the chapter.

4. Select the discussion questions and activities in advance. Feel free to change the order of the listed questions and create your own questions. Allow a set amount of time for the questions and for the activities.

5. Remind your participants that all questions are valid as part of the learning process. Encourage their participation in discussion by saying there are no "wrong" answers and all input will be appreciated. Invite them to share their thoughts, personal stories, and ideas as their comfort level dictates.

6. Some questions may be more difficult to answer than others. If you ask a question and no one responds, begin the discussion by venturing an answer yourself. Then ask for comments and other answers. Remember that some questions may have multiple answers.

7. Ask the question "Why?" or "Why do you believe that?" to help continue a discussion and give it greater depth.

8. Give everyone a chance to talk. Keep the conversation moving. You may want to direct a question at a specific person who has been quiet. "Do you have anything to add?" is a good follow-up question to another person. If the topic of conversation gets off track, move ahead by asking the next question in your leader's guide.

9. Before moving from questions to activities, ask members if they have any questions that have not been answered. Remember that as a leader, you do not have to know all the answers. Some answers will come from group members. Other answers may even need a bit of research. Your role is that of a facilitator, to keep the discussion moving and to encourage participation.

10. Following the conclusion of the activity, close with a brief prayer. If your group desires, pause for individual prayer petitions.

11. Be grateful and supportive. Thank members for their ideas and participation.

12. You are not expected to be a "perfect" leader. Just do the best you can by focusing on helping the participants learn about Christianity. God will help you lead this group.

CHAPTER 1

God the Father Almighty

Chapter Summary

The Apostles' Creed is the universal foundation of Christian faith.

Jesus taught us how God is a father to us.

God has adopted us as his children. He loves us unconditionally.

God's love has liberated us. He gives us freedom of choice.

We are created in the image of God to have a relationship with him.

Discussion Questions

1. What new thought did you have while reading this chapter?
2. What are we looking for when we seek God?
3. How did you first become aware of God?
4. What is your image of God as a father?
5. How does God as our Father meet our needs?
6. What does it mean to believe in God?
7. What does it mean for us that God is all-powerful?
8. How has God shown love for us?
9. In what ways is God's creation an ongoing process?
10. How does our relationship with God liberate us from slavery?
11. Why do you think God allows pain and suffering?
12. What does it mean for us that God loves us unconditionally?

Practical Applications / Activities

1. List ways a human father is similar and different from our heavenly Father.
2. Make a list of the needs of children and discuss how God meets those needs for us, his children.
3. Name some of the responsibilities that go with adoption.

4. As a group project, ask some children to draw pictures of God or tell you about God.
5. List the different ways that God reveals himself to us.

Prayer: *Our Father in heaven, we thank you for making us your children, for loving us and accepting us just the way we are. Help us to remember that we belong to you and that you created us in your image. We ask that you bless this group and continue to open our eyes and ears so that we may learn more about you and your will for us. Be with us during the coming week. We ask this in your holy name. Amen.*

CHAPTER 2

Jesus Christ, God's Only Son, Our Lord

Chapter Summary

> Jesus is God's only Son, our Lord.
> God has come to us in Jesus Christ.
> Christ is the image of God.
> God's promises were fulfilled in Jesus Christ.
> Jesus came to lead us to God.

Discussion Questions

1. What parts of this chapter helped you better understand Jesus?
2. When did you first hear about Jesus?
3. What does the life of Jesus reveal about God?
4. What is the most difficult thing for you to understand about Jesus?
5. What is the least difficult thing for you to understand about Jesus?
6. Why do you think Jesus spoke in parables to express truths?
7. When have you experienced *shalom*, a wholeness or completeness?
8. What prevents us from fully trusting in Jesus?
9. What are people looking for when they seek Jesus?
10. What promises of God did Jesus fulfill?
11. How did our world change because of the life of Jesus?
12. Explain the Incarnation in your own words.

Practical Applications / Activities

1. Examine some children's books about Jesus. What truths do they reveal about Jesus?
2. Contact members or pastors of several different denominations and ask them to briefly explain their faith in Jesus. Compare responses.

3. Look up *Jesus* in a dictionary and an encyclopedia. What do they say?
4. Discuss ways that Christians make Jesus real to others.
5. Create a list of Christian symbols that remind us of Jesus.

Prayer: *Jesus, we thank you for giving us the opportunity to learn more about you and what your life means to us today. Help us to grow in faith so that we may understand your love for us and your will for our lives. Bless this group and watch over us during the coming days so we may return and learn more about you and your love. In your name we pray. Amen.*

CHAPTER 3

Salvation

Chapter Summary

Christ died for our sins to bring us salvation.
We receive God's gift of salvation through faith.
The Cross is the ultimate expression of God's love.
Because of Jesus, God does not count our sins against us.
Justification is the process by which we are made right with God
through God's grace.

Discussion Questions

1. What new insights did you receive from reading this chapter?
2. When have you felt estranged from God? Why?
3. How is the story of Adam and Eve similar to us today?
4. Explain the word *sin* in your own words.
5. What are the consequences of sin?
6. How does it feel to be separated from someone you love?
7. Give some examples of "slavery" that exist today.
8. Why did Jesus die for us?
9. What are the results of salvation through Jesus Christ?
10. Explain what the word *justification* means to you.
11. Give some modern-day examples of reconciliation as it applies
    to our relationships with others.
12. Why does sin separate us from God? What breaks this barrier?

Practical Applications / Activities

1. Make a list of the gifts of God.
2. Ask some children to tell you their definitions of *sin*.
3. Examine the front page of a newspaper to locate "sins" and
   create a list of them along with their causes.
4. As a group, read about and then discuss the first sin as found
   in Genesis 3.

5. Recall some times in your life when you received forgiveness and how you felt afterward.

Prayer: *Heavenly Father, we thank you for coming to us in Jesus to bring us love and forgiveness. Help us to remember all you have done and continue to do in our lives and be thankful for your grace and mercy. Grant us wisdom so we may learn from our mistakes and become better able to serve you. In Jesus' name. Amen.*

CHAPTER 4

The Holy Spirit

Chapter Summary

God is Father, Son, and Holy Spirit.
The Holy Spirit is God at work in human life.
God's gift of the Spirit to us demonstrates we belong to him.
The Holy Spirit empowers us to live as Christians.
The Holy Spirit is Christ alive, indwelling us.

Discussion Questions

1. What insights did you receive from reading this chapter?
2. What is the hardest thing for you to understand about the Trinity?
3. How does the Holy Spirit act on our behalf?
4. Why did God send us the Holy Spirit?
5. What evidence is there that spiritual forces exist?
6. Why does the Holy Spirit convict us of our sins?
7. How does the Holy Spirit help us to cope with life?
8. How does the Holy Spirit help us to forgive?
9. Recall an example of how the Holy Spirit touched your life.
10. In what way is the Holy Spirit a pledge from God to us?
11. How can we tell if the Holy Spirit is with us?
12. How do we speak to and listen to the Holy Spirit in worship?

Practical Applications / Activities

1. Ask a friend to explain the Holy Spirit to you in a few sentences. Write down the response and share it next week with this group.
2. Read and discuss Romans 8:1-16 and share insights about the Holy Spirit.
3. See how the Holy Spirit is depicted in art within several churches and within books on religion.

4. Talk about the Holy Spirit at home or work this week and note people's reactions.
5. Write a list of how the Holy Spirit helps a Christian each day.

Prayer: *Jesus, we thank you for your Holy Spirit, which provides us with your presence every day. Help us to listen to your Spirit so we can serve as your hands and voice in our world today. Allow your Spirit to empower us, to keep us safe, to lead us to repentance, and to share your love with others. In your name we pray. Amen.*

CHAPTER 5

The Church

Chapter Summary

The Church was given birth by the Holy Spirit.
The Church is a gathering of people who have experienced Christ as the risen Lord.
The Church is the body of Christ.
The Spirit that dwells in Jesus dwells in the Church.
The Church is God's idea.

Discussion Questions

1. What new thought did you encounter in this chapter?
2. What are your earliest memories of attending a church?
3. Why has the Church been or not been an important part of your life?
4. What images come to mind when you think of the Church?
5. How does the Church help empower believers?
6. What makes the Church the body of Christ?
7. For what purpose did God give us the Church?
8. Why is the Church called "the house of God" and a home for us?
9. What is worship to the Christian?
10. Why should a Christian attend worship?
11. What is the role of the Holy Spirit within the Church?
12. What characteristics does a vital church have?

Practical Applications / Activities

1. Make a list of ministries of the Church.
2. Discuss the idea of a mission statement for a church.
3. Invite a friend who doesn't attend church to worship with you at your church.
4. Discuss the importance of the music of a worship service.

5. Make a list of what prevents people from attending church.

Prayer: *Dear Lord, we thank you for giving us the Church and the many opportunities we have for ministry. Help us to make the Church a home for everyone, where all are welcome, loved, and accepted. Empower us to become faithful ministers. Open our eyes so we know what needs to be done and remind us that as Christians, we are the Church and a reflection of you. Amen.*

CHAPTER 6

Being Christian

Chapter Summary

Being Christian is being Christ in the world.
Christians grow and learn from their relationship with Christ.
We become "little Christs" by obeying the Holy Spirit.
Compassion is love translated into action.
Christians are related to Christ. They are his disciples.

Discussion Questions

1. What new insights did you receive from this chapter?
2. What Christian traits are seen in the life of Mother Teresa?
3. What Christians have made an impact on your life?
4. What do the images of disciple and pilgrim mean to you?
5. Discuss the demands of Christian discipleship.
6. Why is obedience such an important aspect of being a Christian?
7. What are some of the qualities of a Christian servant?
8. Give some examples of how people are Christian servants.
9. What are some ways Christians can show compassion?
10. In what ways are Christians liberated?
11. How does a person know that he or she belongs to Christ?
12. How do the thoughts and actions of Christians differ from those of non-Christians?

Practical Applications / Activities

1. Make a collection of stories of Christians in action from a national Christian magazine or newspaper.
2. Use a hymnal to locate words that describe a Christian.
3. Make a list of Christian traits for your use as a personal checklist during the day or at night.

4. Interview an elderly Christian in a nursing home about his or her faith.
5. Write a paragraph on the topic "Why I Am a Christian."

Prayer: *Jesus, we thank you for the privilege of being a Christian. We are grateful for the examples of other Christians who share their faith and encourage us. Help us to learn from you and from our Christian brothers and sisters how to share your love with others. We praise you for the many blessings you have given us as your children and ask that you continue to bless and watch over us during the coming week. Amen.*

CHAPTER 7

The Resurrection, Eternal Life, and the Kingdom of God

Chapter Summary

Through his resurrection, Jesus conquered death and guarantees us eternal life.

Nothing can separate us from the love of God in Jesus Christ.

Our eternal life has begun.

God's Kingdom is now. It is a way of life for Christians.

Jesus leads us to the ultimate Promised Land.

Discussion Questions

1. What new thoughts or insights did you encounter in this chapter?
2. When you hear the word *resurrection*, what images come to mind?
3. Recall your first experience of someone's dying.
4. How is Christian immortality different from the natural wish for survival?
5. What do we know about heaven?
6. As Christians, what things do we have to look forward to?
7. What is the kingdom of God?
8. How should Christians handle despair and trouble?
9. What are some differences between physical and spiritual death?
10. Why did God give us eternal life as a gift?
11. What has Jesus told us about the future?
12. What does it mean for you, as a Christian, to have hope?

Practical Applications / Activities

1. Discuss what you have learned from reading this book.
2. Visit a cemetery and note the promises of eternal life written on the tombstones.

3. Ask a child to draw a picture of heaven.
4. Use a hymnal to review hymns sung at funerals. What words of hope are offered?
5. Make a list of some of the promises of God.

Prayer: *Heavenly Father, we thank you for the promise of eternal life and the victory that is ours in Christ. Help us to remember that you are always with us in life and in death. Show us ways to make the most of our precious time on earth so that we may glorify you and further your Kingdom. Thank you for this time together. We ask your blessing as we continue our spiritual journey. In the name of Jesus. Amen.*